PROTECTION BY ANGELS

A

STUDY GUIDE

BY

ELBERT WILLIS

FILL THE GAP PUBLICATIONS
P. O. BOX 53817
LAFAYETTE, LOUISIANA 70505
ISBN: 0-89858-041-2

CONTENTS

FOREWORD

INTRODUCTION

CHAPTER ONE . . .

DESCRIPTION OF ANGELS

      I . . . . .Not All Angels Are Alike

      II . . . . .Angels Are Powerful

      III . . . . .The Number of Angels Is Enormous

      IV . . . . .Not All Angels Are Good

      V . . . . .Angels Have the Ability to Appear as Humans

      VI . . . . .Angels Must Depend Upon God for Victory

CHAPTER TWO . . .

THE MINISTRY OF ANGELS

      I . . . . .Deliverance by Grace

      II . . . . .Deliverance for Faithfulness

      III . . . . .Response to Prayer

      IV . . . . .Provisions

      V . . . . .Guidance

      VI . . . . .Revelations

      VII . . . . .Protection

CHAPTER THREE . . .

CONDITIONS FOR ANGEL PROTECTION

I . . . . Computer Reprogramming

II . . . . Constant Contact

III . . . . Continuous Confession

IV . . . . Confidence in the Word

V . . . . Complete Love

VI . . . . Comprehend the Power of Jesus' Name

CHAPTER FOUR . . .
AREAS OF ANGEL PROTECTION

I . . . . Evils from Which Deliverance Is Promised

II . . . . Reward of Those Who Trust God

CHAPTER FIVE . . .
INCREASING LIFE'S SPAN

I . . . . Know God's Plan

II . . . . Know God's Conditions

III . . . . Know God Is the Real Source of Health and Life

IV . . . . Know Where Strength Comes From

V . . . . Know Faith Must Be Operative to Reap the Benefits

CHAPTER SIX . . .
MAINTAINING PROTECTION

I . . . . Consistent Meditation for Mind Renewal

II . . . . Consistent Confession for Faith Operation

III . . . . Stop Thinking Fear Possibilities or Suppositions

IV . . . . Stop Talking Fear

V . . . . Act in Ways that Demonstrate Trust and Confidence in God

FOREWORD
DIVINE PROTECTION

Psalm 34:7, "The angel of the Lord encampeth round about them that fear Him, and delivereth them."

Psalm 84:11, "For the Lord God is a sun and shield: the Lord will give grace and glory: no good thing will he withhold from them that walk uprightly."

Psalm 90:10, "The days of our years are threescore years and ten; and if by reason of strength they be fourscore years . . ."

Psalm 91:10, "There shall no evil befall thee, neither shall any plague come nigh thy dwelling."

Psalm 91:11-12, "For he shall give his angels charge over thee, to keep thee in all thy ways. They shall bear thee up in their hands, lest thou dash thy foot against a stone."

Psalm 115:11, "Ye that fear the Lord, trust in the Lord: He is their help and their shield."

Psalm 121:7, "The Lord shall preserve thee from all evil."

Proverbs 2:8, "He keepeth the paths of judgment, and preserveth the way of his saints."

Proverbs 2:10-12, "When wisdom entereth into thine heart, and knowledge is pleasant unto thy soul; Discretion shall preserve thee, understanding shall keep thee: To deliver thee from the way of the evil

1

man, from the man that speaketh froward things."

Proverbs 3:1-2, "My son, forget not my law; but let thine heart keep my commandments: for length of days, and long life, and peace, shall they add to thee."

Proverbs 4:10, "Hear, O my son, and receive my sayings; and the years of thy life shall be many."

Proverbs 9:11, "For by me thy days shall by multiplied, and the years of thy life shall be increased."

Proverbs 10:27, "The fear of the Lord prolongeth days: but the years of the wicked shall be shortened."

Proverbs 11:8, "The righteous is delivered out of trouble, and the wicked cometh in his stead."

Proverbs 14:3, "The lips of the wise shall preserve them."

Proverbs 30:5, "Every word of God is pure: he is a shield unto them that put their trust in him."

Luke 10:19, "Behold, I give unto you power to tread on serpents and scorpions, and over all the power of the enemy: and nothing shall by any means hurt you."

John 17:15, "I pray not that thou shouldest take them out of the world, but that thou shouldest keep them from the evil."

John 17:20, "Neither pray I for thee alone, but for them also which shall believe on me through their word."

II Thessalonians 3:2-3, "And that we may be delivered from unreasonable and wicked men: for all men have not faith. But the Lord is faithful, who shall establish you, and keep you from evil."

II Timothy 4:17-18, "Notwithstanding the Lord stood with me, and strengthened me; that by me the preaching might be fully known . . . and I was delivered out of the mouth of the lion. And the Lord shall deliver me from every evil work, and will preserve me unto his heavenly kingdom."

INTRODUCTION

As a Baptist pastor for many years I didn't know anything about angels. I pictured angels as being about two feet tall, with little rosy cheeks and a harp, and flying around playing cupid. That was my concept of angels. This concept hindered our faith in believing for God's angels to encamp around us, and protect us. About eight years ago as I began to meditate on divine healing, I began to realize how many people's lives were snuffed out before they were able to finish their work. I began to seek God about these things, and it was during that time I ran across various Scriptures about angels. Then I began to hear other men of God talking about protection by angels; and I heard some teaching on Psalm 91, and it began to stir inside me. So I researched the Scriptures and began to meditate on them, and to confess the Scriptures, and it just came to be a reality that I knew in my heart that angels were really, really, really real. They are spirit beings. You can't see them with your natural eye, but through discernment of the spirit, or many times a revelation from God, you can see them; or they can manifest themselves in the natural so you can see them.

I began to realize that God's angels really existed and they were God's protection force to guard God's people, and that is when I came to the place where I cancelled all my insurance. I felt like insurance was man's method of protection and it couldn't keep something from happening, it just helped you after it happened. I began to realize that God had angels to take care of His children, that would keep things from happening to them that other people would still be struggling with. As you learn about God's Word and about the protection of angels, you can ward off this evil from happening to you and also from happening to your family. The Lord has dealt with me strongly concerning angels. I have lived for years trusting in the angels of the Lord to take care of me, and my family.

Many times as I was driving along the highway, all at once, with my spiritual eyes, I could see angels sitting on the front of my car. As I would look in my mirror, I could see them sitting on the back of my car. Not too long ago I was driving along and I looked out the side window, and an angel was sitting on air, right beside me — only outside the car. I looked at him, and he smiled at me. I thought to myself, I wonder what he's smiling so much about, and the Lord spoke to me and said, "Son, because you believe in them, you give them something to do." God has been dealing with me strongly in the past year concerning angels, because we're going to come into some rough, tough days, and we will need God's protection. The devil is out to destroy God's people. The devil hates everybody, but especially Christians; and he'd rather destroy you and stop your witness more than anyone else, because you are representing Jesus. You're out there witnessing, you're out there as a potential threat to him by telling someone about Jesus. I just want to encourage you, as you study these chapters, to really get hold of the Scriptures and be diligent, because the angels of the Lord protect you, your family, and your possessions.

Let me share this testimony concerning angels.

4

During the time I was taking lessons to learn how to fly an airplane, the instructor was going to teach me the stall principle. Whey you stall an airplane you pull the nose all the way up and the wind does not flow over the wings, and the plane begins to fall. My instructor told me to start pulling the controls back. I started pulling it back, and I pulled it nearly all the way; and I heard the stall buzzer and I let off a little bit. The instructor said, "No, pull it all the way back." So I did, but the plane just would not completely stall. The instructor told me again to pull it all the way back, but I already had it back all the way. The instructor then took the controls and attempted to stall the plane, but it would not stall. He kept saying it would fall any time, but it would not. I'll never forget — I looked out to my left, and I looked out to my right, and I saw an angel on each wing of that airplane. I just kind of laughed, realizing that God was taking care of me. My flight instructor looked at me and said, "What's wrong?" I said, "Man, you aren't going to stall this thing today." He said, "What do you mean?" I said, "There's an angel on both wings." I just kind of spit it out before I thought about it, and he just looked at me, and lowered the nose back down. I guarantee you that pilot never ran across anything like that before. I am coming more and more to know the reality of angels. I praise God for His protecting angels, because we can sleep, and rest, and do many other things because we trust in them.

Many times we have had our children come to us and say, "I saw an angel." When they tell you they saw one, you talk to them a little bit and get them to tell you about it. I've heard many, many children talk about seeing angels, and I believe they saw them. We've missed some blessings by not believing in angels.

CHAPTER ONE

DESCRIPTION OF ANGELS
OUTLINE

INTRODUCTION:

Angels have a two-fold ministry:

1. Messengers: Represent God's interest
   - Help carry out the plan and will of God.
2. Protectors: Psalm 121:7, "The Lord shall preserve thee from all evil." Psalm 34:7; Psalm 91:11.

I. NOT ALL ANGELS ARE ALIKE:

1. Archangels: Michael, chief messenger. Daniel 10:21; 12:1.
2. Special messenger: Gabriel. Daniel 8:16; 9:21; Luke 1:13.
3. Cherubims: Genesis 3:24, as guards of His.
4. Seraphims: Isaiah 6:2 - Six wings, face and feet.
5. Guardian angels: Matthew 18:10.

II. ANGELS ARE POWERFUL:

1. Genesis 19:11, smote men at door with blindness.
2. II Kings 19:35, killed 185,000 Assyrians.
3. Acts 12:7-11, "chains fell off Peter's hands . . . jail."

III. THE NUMBER OF ANGELS IS ENORMOUS:

Hebrews 12:22 "To an innumerable company of angels."

Revelation 5:11, "And the number of them was ten thousand times ten thousand, and thousands of thousands."

IV. NOT ALL ANGELS ARE GOOD:

II Corinthians 11:13-14, "Satan himself is changed into an angel of light."

V. ANGELS HAVE THE ABILITY TO APPEAR AS HUMANS:

1. Genesis 18:2, "Looked, and, lo, three men stood by him." 18:2, "Did eat."
2. Acts 10:30, "Behold, a man stood before me in bright clothing."
3. Hebrews 13:2, "Be not forgetful to entertain strangers, for thereby . . ."

VI. ANGELS MUST DEPEND UPON GOD FOR VICTORY: Jude 9.

"Michael said, The Lord rebuke thee."

VII. OTHER BRIEF AIDS TO UNDERSTANDING ANGELS:

1. Masculine in gender.
2. Immortal: Luke 20:36, "Neither can they die any more: for they are equal unto the angels."
3. Names: Gabriel, Michael, Lucifer.
4. Do not marry: Matthew 22:30, "In the resurrection they neither marry, nor are given in marriage, but are as the angels of God in heaven." Blows theory of man and angels mating.
5. Created by God — they are not children of God. Ezekiel 28:15, "From the day that thou wast created."
6. Not dead saints, since created.

CHAPTER ONE
DESCRIPTION OF ANGELS

INTRODUCTION: Primarily, the ministry of angels is two-fold. First, they are messengers. They represent God's interests. They help carry out the plan and the will of God. We will see later that God created them, and they are His messengers. Many times in the Bible they appear to God's servants in times of need, and circumstances and situations.

Secondly, they are protectors. **Psalm 121:7** says, "THE LORD SHALL PRESERVE THEE FROM ALL EVIL." Psalm 34:7 is the Scripture that many Christians are familiar with, "THE ANGEL OF THE LORD ENCAMPETH ROUND ABOUT THEM THAT FEAR HIM (reverence Him, believe in Him), AND DELIVERETH THEM." **Psalm 91:11,** "FOR HE SHALL GIVE HIS ANGELS CHARGE OVER, THEE, TO KEEP THEE IN ALL THY WAYS." You need to believe in those angels, because you are going to need them to protect your sons and daughters. You won't have to live in fear, if you have your faith operating for God's angels to encamp round about them.

I. **NOT ALL ANGELS ARE ALIKE.** Let's look at some various things that will describe these particular angels. There are five brief divisions.

1. Archangels. Michael is the chief messenger. We find

this in **Daniel 10:21; 12:1.** Many feel that Michael will have a lot to do with end time activity.

2. Special messenger, which is Gabriel. We find reference to him in Daniel 8:16 and 9:21; and also in Luke the first chapter, because Gabriel came to Mary and then to Joseph. In many places in the Bible Gabriel was a special messenger.

3. Cherubims. **Genesis 3:24,** after Adam and Eve were cast out of the garden, these cherubims stood at the gates of the garden of Eden. Read **Ezekiel 10:1-2;** it describes them. In one particular place it talks about their having four faces and four sets of wheels, etc. What it is saying is that they can go any direction quickly. They are mobile; they can go quickly to do the things of God. Cherubims were assigned to keep Adam and Eve out of the garden of Eden.

4. Seraphims: **Isaiah 6:2.** It says they have six wings, a face and feet, and with two of their wings they fly.

5. Guardian angels: **Matthew 18:10,** ''TAKE HEED THAT YE DESPISE NOT ONE OF THESE LITTLE ONES; FOR I SAY UNTO YOU, THAT IN HEAVEN THEIR ANGELS DO ALWAYS BEHOLD THE FACE OF MY FATHER WHICH IS IN HEAVEN.''

These are briefly the five types of angels. Some Bible scholars and teachers give more divisions than five, but most all of them break them down into at least five kinds of angels. Primarily, we are going to be dealing with the guardian angels, the angels that are assigned by God to protect His people. In chapter two we will see that angels are ministering spirits sent forth by God to minister unto them that are heirs of salvation. Everything that God does is by faith. Believe, by faith, that angels are real and that God sends them to minister to you.

In earlier days I didn't see angels, but I began to believe in them stronger and stronger, and now I wake up in the morning and look out my window and my ministering angel is right there. He looks over and smiles at me. You may think I'm crazy, but that's all right — he's there. Regardless of what anyone believes, I know he's there. There have been times when I was flying on a jet airliner, 30,000 feet above the earth, and I looked out the little window and my guardian angel was right there. The height doesn't bother him, or the speed of jets doesn't affect him either. Angels are on the earth, ministering for those who are heirs of salvation. Praise the Lord!

II. **ANGELS ARE POWERFUL:** Angels are powerful and strong. In **Genesis 19:11** we find that the angels came to Abraham, and then two of them went into the city of Sodom. When they went in to Sodom, and walked down the streets, they appeared like men. They went into Lot's house, and that night the men of the city came to take them. The Scripture says that they smote the men at the door with blindness — they are powerful. All the men that gathered at the door of Lot's house were stricken with blindness.

In **II Kings 19:35,** one angel killed 185,000 Assyrians. Now that's one angel. The Bible says Jesus could have called 10,000 angels — do you believe He would have had Him an army? 10,000, and each one of them could have killed 185,000, and maybe some of them more. Hallelujah! Let's look at **II Kings 19:35,** "AND IT CAME TO PASS THAT NIGHT, THAT THE ANGEL OF THE LORD WENT OUT, AND SMOTE IN THE CAMP OF THE ASSYRIANS AN HUNDRED FOURSCORE AND FIVE THOUSAND: AND WHEN THEY AROSE EARLY IN THE MORNING, BEHOLD, THEY WERE ALL DEAD CORPSES." Saints, that's power. They have power that you and I have never comprehended. A lady in the church I pastored a few years ago told of an experience she had while driving down the

11

highway, accompanied by another sister in the Lord. Somewhere along the highway they had to stop real quickly, and as they stopped there was a huge tandem truck behind them. She said she saw in her mirror the truck bearing down on her car, and realized there was no way it could stop. All at once it hit, but they didn't feel anything. The truck driver got out of his truck scratching his head. He couldn't figure out how in the world that big truck hit her car and didn't dent it or damage anything. He hit something that felt like a rock. He hit a rock, all right! An angel! Those ladies believe in angels. We need to realize that they are powerful as they minister on behalf of Believers.

In **Acts 12:7-11** Peter was in jail. The angel came in, and the chains fell off Peter's hands; and the angel let him out of the jail, and the gates opened without help. He came and delivered Peter. I'm just giving you a few examples to help you understand that they are powerful. Believe in their power to protect you.

III. **THE NUMBER OF ANGELS IS ENORMOUS. Hebrews 12:22** says, "TO AN INNUMERABLE COMPANY OF ANGELS." **Revelation 5:11,** "AND THE NUMBER OF THEM WAS TEN THOUSAND TIMES TEN THOUSAND, AND THOUSANDS OF THOUSANDS." Do you have any idea what that number is? When Lucifer rebelled and there was war in heaven, a third of the angels were banned from heaven. That leaves two thirds of the angels on God's side, and gives us two-to-one odds. Two thirds of them were faithful, and what are they doing? Sitting in heaven playing their harps? No, they are about the Master's business. They were created by Him to help Him run this universe. He's using them as His lieutenants. There are billions of people in this world; that's nothing compared to the number of angels. Saints, they have the whole universe to run around in. We are limited to this earth at the present time, a few airplanes in the sky and a few rockets reaching beyond gravity; but the angels of God have the entire universe to travel in. They are spiritual beings, all over the universe.

IV. **NOT ALL ANGELS ARE GOOD.** We just mentioned something about that. **II Corinthians 11:13-14** says, ". . . SATAN HIMSELF IS CHANGED INTO AN ANGEL OF LIGHT." We know that he rebelled against God, he was cast out, and he deceived Adam and Eve in the garden. They turned their dominion over to him. It says in Genesis that God gave to Adam and Eve dominion over everything on the earth: over the fish, the fowls of the air, the animals, everything. Adam and Eve had dominion. But they sold it to Lucifer. But, praise be to God, Jesus came and bought it back. Jesus came and defeated the devil. He defeated Lucifer, and through Jesus Christ's defeat of Satan He has now brought back, to the Believer, the dominion of all the things in the world, if we will operate in faith and believe it. Part of this dominion is beginning to recognize the power the angels have been given.

V. **ANGELS HAVE THE ABILITY TO APPEAR AS HUMANS.** In **Genesis 18:2-8** Abraham "LOOKED, AND, LO, THREE MEN STOOD BY HIM . . . AND THEY DID EAT." He went and fixed something, and they did eat. **Acts 10:30** says, "BEHOLD, A MAN STOOD BEFORE ME IN BRIGHT CLOTHING." Go to the Scriptures and you see very plainly it says they were angels, but they appeared as humans. **Hebrews 13:2** says, "BE NOT FORGETFUL TO ENTERTAIN STRANGERS: FOR THEREBY SOME HAVE ENTERTAINED ANGELS UNAWARES." They have the ability to appear in human form. I'm just giving you two or three instances, but it's all through the Bible that they appeared in human form. We find many times that they did not appear in human form, but when they appeared they were very clearly recognized and it was known that they were angels. I know one of the reasons that **we** are protected so much is because we truly believe in them. I'm talking about really believing that they are there; really believing that they are guarding you and your family, and your property, and really believing that wherever you are, the guardian angels are going right along with you.

I've never had one to appear to me as a human, but I would surely like to have that experience, wouldn't you? I have plenty of Scripture that says they are sent to protect you and me from all evil; and there is evil in this world, **and** we need protection. You can try every way in the world, but why strain yourself when one angel is powerful enough to kill 185,000 men? God can assign a few of them to you if you will believe in them. You don't need but one, but if you have two or three, you are well taken care of. The angels are the Christian's garment of protection. I want to encourage you as you go through this study guide to get the Scriptures and meditate on them, and start confessing with your mouth, "I believe in angels." When I first started confessing it, I felt like a fool. You know, you weren't supposed to believe in angels; it was kind of ridiculous. Especially if you thought they were going to protect you. I saw them outside my house for a long, long time before I told anybody. I'd been seeing them for a long, long time before I ever said it.

Realize they have the ability to appear as humans, and be open to receive "heavenly strangers."

VI. **ANGELS MUST DEPEND UPON GOD FOR VICTORY.** In **Jude 9** it says Michael said unto Lucifer, "THE LORD REBUKE THEE." You see, they are so powerful that one could kill 185,000 men; but still they have to trust in God. God is their creator; He's still the source of their well-being, just as He is yours and mine. Do

14

not forget they will never get to the place where they don't have to trust in God. Even if one angel killed 185,000 men, that angel is still subject unto God. They are mighty and they are powerful, but they're not in the same category as God. We need to realize they are just created beings that God made to be His messengers, and to protect Christians from the evil in this world that is getting worse and worse all the time. Ladies, you don't have to live under fear if you will start trusting God's angels; you don't have to be so fearful about your daughters being raped, if you learn to trust in God's angels. Men, you won't have to be so fearful about someone breaking into your house, if you learn to trust in God's angels. Children, you won't have to be so fearful about something happening to Daddy and to Mama, if you learn to trust in God's angels. Saints, it will give you a fresh peace, and a comfort, just to know "God has His angels to protect me and my family, and if God's angels can't do it I'm wasting my time worrying about trying to do it."

VII. **OTHER BRIEF AIDS TO UNDERSTANDING ANGELS.** Let's look at some brief aids to help us understand some questions you may have wondered about.

1. Masculine in gender. Every time angels are named in the Bible, they are masculine.

2. Immortal. Angels are immortal. **Luke 20:36** says, "NEITHER CAN THEY DIE ANY MORE: FOR THEY ARE EQUAL UNTO THE ANGELS." This Scripture refers to people at the resurrection. Jesus says, "NEITHER CAN THEY DIE ANY MORE: FOR THEY ARE EQUAL UNTO THE ANGELS." There will come a time when men will not die any more. That will make us equal to the angels, because angels cannot die; they are immortal.

3. Names. Angels have names: Gabriel, Michael, Lucifer. Not many names of angels are mentioned in the Bible, but personally I believe every angel has a name.

4. They do not marry. **Matthew 22:30** says, "IN THE RESURRECTION THEY NEITHER MARRY, NOR ARE GIVEN IN MARRIAGE, BUT ARE AS THE ANGELS OF GOD IN HEAVEN." Now, this blows the theory of men and angels mating. You know there is a concept in the Book of Genesis that the fallen angels mated with the earthly women and brought forth giant men in that particular day and time, but if they are not able to marry I don't see how they are able to produce life.

5. They are created by God; they are not children of God. **Ezekiel 28:15** says, "FROM THE DAY THAT THOU WAST CREATED." Many people think angels may be children of God, dead saints now serving as angels. It is amazing, the concepts people have concerning angels. They are not born of God; they are created by God. They can't call God, Father; they are not sons of God. Believers are the sons of God. They have their position; they have their tasks, and they have their work; and their primary ministry is being messengers, bringing forth direction that God wants His children to know. From testimonies of men in past years, when they learned specific truths that enabled them to come into some mighty areas with God, the angels of God appeared unto them and revealed things to them. I believe that the angels of God are messengers. They were sent to Mary, Joseph, and Zacharias. Many places in the Bible tell about angels being sent by God to give particular messages. I believe that God in these last days will use His angels. He is going to send them to His people, and give them special instructions that will help them to move into the mighty manifestation of the glory and the power of the living God. The message of the angels that come from God to bring any kind of information or direction to Believers will **always** line up with the Word of God. If an angel is sent from God, whatever he says will always line up with what God says. If in a dream,

or in a vision, you have an appearance of an angelic being, listen carefully to what he says; and have your spirit so in tune with God that even in a dream you can say, "I hear you, but I'm going to check you out." Suppose it is God? God doesn't mind your checking Him out, but the devil will get mad if you say you're going to check him out. I've seen some times in earlier days when I would get some mighty strong thoughts in my mind to do things, and when the thought persisted I would say aloud: "Boy, that thought is surely strong. That seems like it may be God, but you know what I'm going to do? I'm just going to sit on it for a few days, and check it out in the Word." The next thing I knew, that thought would start pushing me, "If you don't do it now you're going to miss it." That gave me my answer: God doesn't hurry, or rush me into things. In the name of Jesus I rebuked that thought. That thought would not return again.

Remember, the angels are there to protect you, but at the same time the angels of light are going to try to deceive you, and lead you astray.

I want you to make this confession: "In the name of Jesus, I confess that I'm open to the truth of God's Word about angels as messengers of God. And, Father God, I want You to know I am willing to receive any message from Your angels, but at the same time I confess in Jesus' name I will not receive any message from any angels that are not from God. And I confess in Jesus' name that I am going to learn the Word of God that teaches the protection ministry of angels; because I want to be protected, and I want my family protected, and I want our possessions protected. Therefore, I am going to learn God's Word, so my faith can operate; because faith must have the Word to stand upon. So I will learn the Word of God about angels. Amen."

***

CHAPTER TWO
MINISTRY OF ANGELS

OUTLINE

I.   DELIVERANCE BY GRACE

II.   DELIVERANCE FOR FAITHFULNESS

III.   RESPONSE TO PRAYER

IV.   PROVISIONS

V.   GUIDANCE

VI.   REVELATIONS

VIII.   PROTECTION

CHAPTER TWO
MINISTRY OF ANGELS

In this chapter we will consider the ministry of angels. **Romans 10:17,** "FAITH COMETH BY HEARING, AND HEARING BY THE WORD OF GOD." When I first began to teach faith a number of years ago, some people had difficulty in getting hold of faith, but as they learned the Word it began to operate for them. Divine healing, financial prosperity, deliverance, living in victory every day — in whatever area you need to move into faith, you must know the Word of God.

Hebrews 1:14 says, "ARE THEY NOT ALL MINISTERING SPIRITS, SENT FORTH TO MINISTER FOR THEM WHO SHALL BE HEIRS OF SALVATION?" This Scripture says the ministering spirits are sent forth on behalf of those who are the heirs of salvation — that is you and me. God has sent His ministering spirits, His angels, to deliver messages and to protect His own. I'm convinced more than ever before that as we begin to move into the years ahead, we are going to need to know the Word of God on protection by angels, because the enemy is going to continually be trying to defeat and destroy God's people. Most angels are not very busy, because they are not being used. I'll never forget when I first started studying faith about eight years ago, I was praying about all kinds of things, and kind of got embarrassed because I felt like I was asking God for too many things. The Lord spoke to me and said, "Son, I'm not busy." I said, "What do You mean, You're not busy; all these people praying?" He said, "They are not praying in faith. Many are praying, but all I answer is the prayer of faith. I'm not busy." There are not very many people who know how to pray the prayer of faith. God began to show me years ago some things concerning His angels. By the grace of God they are doing **some** things, but they are not very busy because most of God's people don't believe in them. They don't believe they will protect them, because they don't know the Word of God. **II Corinthians 2:11** says, ". . . WE ARE NOT IGNORANT OF HIS (Satan's) DEVICES . . ." Saints, we haven't just been ignorant about angels, we have been stupid. We have been illiterates concerning them.

In chapter one we observed their attributes. In this chapter we are going to discover various ways angels assist God's people. God created them to administrate the universe for Himself, and to be sent forth by Him to deliver messages, and to be sent forth by Him to minister to His people, to protect and take care of them. God knows that the devil wants to kill every single one of us (John 10:10), and we need divine power to protect us; and glory to God, the power of God's angels is that protecting power we have available.

I.   **DELIVERANCE BY GRACE.** This is one of the ways angels assist God's people. I call it "Deliverance by Grace." Many times when you and I were not even believing God, when we probably should have been dead, should have been killed, we said we were "lucky." I want to tell you what it was; I believe it was grace, pure unmerited grace. I want to refer to one passage concerning this: **Genesis 19:16** talks about Lot. Lot was in Sodom. He

22

had separated himself from Abraham and was living in this wicked city, yet God loved him so much He sent the angels there to bring him out, even though the Scripture says he lingered. The angels told Lot what was going to happen, and said, "Lot, let's get out of here." The Scripture says he lingered, and the Lord was still merciful unto him. You and I lingered a long time out in the world. Now, since we've been to Jesus, we lingered about believing in angels. People say angels are folklore, fantasy, fairy tale, mystic, a figment of the imagination. But the Lord, being merciful unto Lot, brought him forth. It doesn't say how he brought him forth. It wouldn't surprise me at all if the angels carried him out. **Genesis 19:16** reads: "THE LORD BEING MERCIFUL UNTO HIM: AND THEY BROUGHT HIM FORTH, AND SET HIM WITHOUT THE CITY." I don't know how you are going to "set" someone without the city if you don't pick him up and carry him out. That hit me when I read the passage. I had never thought about it before. If one angel could kill 185,000 men, surely two could pick up two or three people and set them outside a city. With the power they have, which we talked about in chapter one, where one of them killed 185,000 men, it would be no problem for them to pick up Lot and his family and set them outside the city. This is what I call "deliverance by grace," and I want to thank God for the many times He delivered me by unmerited grace. I believe if He hadn't, every single one of us would be dead. I believe in deliverance by grace. But you know, if there is deliverance by **grace,** just think what we can have by **faith.** God loves us so much, and desires to see people come to know Him, that I believe those angels are continually protecting people whom Satan tries to destroy, but God's grace reaches out through His angels and delivers. When you and I come to the knowledge of God, and the knowledge of His Word, then we can exercise faith for

23

God's angels to protect us every time, in every situation, and every circumstance. Praise the Lord!

II. **DELIVERANCE FOR FAITHFULNESS.** In **Acts 5:19** we observe, "THE ANGEL OF THE LORD BY NIGHT OPENED THE PRISON DOORS." The apostles were put in prison for preaching the Gospel! That's a good reason to be in prison. You know what's a good reason to have people angry and mad at you? Preaching the Gospel. You know what's a good reason to be persecuted? Preaching the Gospel. You know what's a good reason to have people mocking and ridiculing you? Preaching the Gospel. You know what's a good reason to have people shying away from you? Preaching the Gospel. "THE ANGEL OF THE LORD BY NIGHT OPENED THE PRISON DOORS." It doesn't say the angel used a key. "AND BROUGHT THEM FORTH, AND SAID, GO, STAND AND SPEAK IN THE TEMPLE . . ." They were put in prison for preaching, but the angel opened the door, brought them out and said, "O,K. fellows; go, stand, and preach it again." They said, "We can't help but tell what we have seen and heard." When that fire of the Holy Ghost begins to burn inside of you, you can't help but tell it. As you are faithful to proclaim the Word of God, His angels will guard and protect you. If you will preach that Gospel and share the Word, the Bible says through the foolishness of preaching, teaching, and sharing the Word of God, many shall be saved. Glory to God. It is every believer's privilege and responsibility to preach the Gospel. What is the Gospel? The good news that Jesus **saves** all who come unto Him. What's the good news? That Jesus **heals** all who come. What's the good news? That Jesus **delivers** all who come; He **prospers** all who come, and gives **victory** to all those who come. Go, stand, and preach, wherever you are. Testify of the glory of your Lord and Saviour, Jesus Christ.

Acts 12:7-11 records that Peter was in prison. He was asleep, and the angel came and touched him, and shook him and told him to wake up. The angel then led him out of the prison to freedom. Peter thought he was dreaming until he got outside. The angel of the Lord came because Peter was faithful. Why was Peter in prison? Do you suppose it was because of some secret sin? Do you know what got the apostles in prison? Preaching the gospel of Jesus Christ! Do you know what will get you in trouble with the devil, and with people? Preaching Jesus. You can talk about **God** and it doesn't bother anybody, but you start using that Name that is above every name, that Name of Jesus, and it will get you in trouble. If you get in trouble for preaching Jesus, get ready for a miracle, because you are then in miracle land. If you're willing to pay the price to take the ridicule and the mockery of the world for preaching Jesus, get ready for a miracle, because that's the kind God gives miracles to! Glory to God. I believe preaching Jesus will put you in miracle land to get physical, mental, and financial miracles quicker than anything else; because you will be standing and proclaiming that Name of Jesus. It worked for the early Apostles, and since God is no respecter of persons, it works today for those who continue to proclaim the Name of Jesus.

In **Acts 27:23-24** there was a storm at sea. They threw everything overboard. The natural situation looked bad. The Scripture says that Paul was absent for a little while. Paul was down in the ship praying, then he came back on deck and told them, ". . . I EXHORT YOU TO BE OF GOOD CHEER: FOR THERE SHALL BE NO LOSS OF ANY MAN'S LIFE AMONG YOU, BUT OF THE SHIP. FOR THERE STOOD BY ME THIS NIGHT THE ANGEL OF GOD, WHOSE I AM, AND WHOM I SERVE." Who gave Paul this information? The angel of God. This deliverance was because of Paul's faithfulness. Paul was faithful to

God. Before they left on that voyage, Paul was faithful to warn them. He said, "I perceive there's going to be trouble on this voyage." He told them, and they laughed at him; they didn't pay him any mind. But when they found themselves in trouble, and were about to die, and Paul came up from the lower part of the ship and said the angel of God appeared to him, there is no indication they laughed any more. They were ready to believe anything. Because Paul was faithful, the angel of God appeared to him to give him direction and encouragement. Being faithful to God will deliver you. I've seen times when it looked like I was about to have an accident, or something was about to happen to me, and all at once it didn't happen. Some say, "Brother Willis, you're just lucky." I don't believe in luck. I believe one of God's angels was right there.

III. **RESPONSE TO PRAYER. Genesis 21:17** says, "AND GOD HEARD THE VOICE OF THE LAD; AND THE ANGEL OF GOD CALLED TO HAGAR." Abraham sent Hagar and Ishmael away. They went out into the middle of the desert. They were dying because they had no water. The heat and desert conditions were getting them, and the lad, the boy Ishmael, called; and it says God heard his voice and He spoke to Hagar. As you read the story, it says that her eyes were opened and there was water right there. I wonder how that water just "happened" to get there all at once. It says all at once her eyes were opened and the water was right there. You know what? Her eyes were probably closed just long enough for God to do a miracle right there in the middle of the desert. You may say, "Well, Brother Willis, it could have been there all along." Well, it could have been there, but it could have been a miracle, too. I'm saying God can put an oasis in the middle of the desert.

Isaiah 37:15, 35-36 says Hezekiah prayed unto the Lord, and then the prophet came to him and told him God said, "I will defend this city," and the angel of the Lord smote 185,000 Assyrians. They were boxed in by the Assyrians. Hezekiah prayed, and the prophet of God came to him with the message that God would defend the city. God says He will defend **you,** He says He will take care of **you,** because you are precious to Him. You are now the children of God, heirs of God and joint-heirs with Jesus Christ. If He protected those in the Old Testament in their relationship, you can be assured you and I are in a good position, if we'll begin to believe God to send His angels to minister in behalf of His children.

In the **first chapter of Luke** it says that Zacharias and his wife Elisabeth were righteous people before God; they followed Him and obeyed all the things of God. But, it said, Elisabeth was without child. Zacharias was in the temple one day and the angel of God said unto him, "Zacharias, God has heard your prayer, and I have come here to tell you that your wife Elisabeth is going to have a son." Their son was John the Baptist, the forerunner who proclaimed that Jesus Christ was coming. So we see the angels of God do appear in response to prayer. **John 16:23** says that whatsoever you ask the Father in the name of Jesus, He will do it.

IV. **PROVISIONS.** This is another way that angels help God's people — with provisions. **I Kings 19:5-7** records the story of the angel providing for God's prophet Elijah. "THE ANGEL SAID . . . ARISE AND EAT." The first time Elijah woke up, he saw fire and some cooking going on. Evidently he went back to sleep, he was so tired. He slept a little while longer while the food was being cooked, then the angel shook him again and said, "Arise and eat." The angel said, "The journey you are going to make is great for thee, so arise and eat." The Bible says he "WENT IN THE STRENGTH OF THAT MEAT FORTY DAYS AND FORTY NIGHTS." I'd like to have a meal like that. Believers today had better believe these things, because when it gets rough the angels of God can bring you some food that will take you forty days and forty nights! Yes, there are going to be times like this. I'll never forget a vision God gave me a few years ago. My family was seated at the dinner table; the plates were there before us, empty. I bowed my head and prayed. When I opened my eyes, food would be on the plates. All during the day and night people were breaking into our house looking for food. I would look out the window and see the people outside, and they were skinny. We were healthy, and they were skinny. So they would see us and they were sure that we had to be hiding food. We would just keep telling them, "God gives it to us; God gives it to us." They would say, "Aw, we don't believe that. You've got it hidden around here somewhere." They were just tearing our house upside down, everywhere. We would bow our heads and pray, and thank God for the food; we would open our eyes, and food would be on the plates. In the vision God was providing — one meal at a time.

When God impressed me a few months ago to start teaching this series on angels, He said, "Son, My people need to get the Word in them concerning the protection of My angels; they are going to **need** it." You need it now, saints; but there is going to come a time shortly that you are going to need it more and more. Let me tell you how the Antichrist and devil are going to work in the world in the end time. He's going to come through public utilities. They will come to you and say, "You're going to take this mark or we're going to cut off your electricity." It may be in the cold of winter. "We'll cut your electricity off; we'll cut your gas off; we'll cut your water off; we'll cut your sewage off." How are you going to make it? Listen to me, Saints. This is one of the ways they are going to require you take the mark of the beast. You can just imagine right now if they came and said, "We are going to cut off your electricity, cut off your water, cut off your gas, and cut off your sewage" — how could you live in a house in the system that we are in today if you don't know how to believe God? What will you do?

V. **GUIDANCE, II KINGS 1:15** says, "AND THE ANGEL OF THE LORD SAID UNTO ELIJAH, GO DOWN WITH HIM: BE NOT AFRAID." God wanted Elijah to go to a certain place but he didn't want to go. The angel came to him and said, "Hey, Elijah, go on down and don't be afraid." I wonder why he told him — you reckon he would be by himself? No! The angels would be there. No need to be afraid when you are travelling, when you recognize God's angels are there. You don't have to be tormented by fear, when you believe that God's angels are real and they will protect you.

In **Matthew 1:20,** "THE ANGEL OF THE LORD AP-PEARED . . . SAYING, JOSEPH, ... TAKE UNTO THEE MARY THY WIFE: FOR THAT WHICH IS CONCEIVED IN HER IS OF THE HOLY GHOST." Mary came up pregnant, and Joseph said, "Hey, I don't want her." In that day an engagement was more solid than a marriage today. They were engaged for one year, and then they were married. During this time, before they were married, Mary became pregnant. Joseph got a little upset — a little disturbed; and I can understand why. Then the angel of God gave his guidance. The angel came unto him and said, "Joseph, marry her. That which is conceived in her is of the Holy Ghost, born of the Holy Spirit of the Living God." Saints, that's guidance; and God will guide you when you need decisions in the things of life.

In **Matthew 2:13** we find that after Jesus was born, the angel of God came to Joseph in a dream and said, "TAKE THE YOUNG CHILD . . . AND FLEE INTO EGYPT." King Herod was getting ready to kill all the babies two years of age and under, in order to kill the "king of the Jews." The angel of the Lord gave Joseph specific instructions for the situation at hand.

In **Matthew 2:21** they went back to Israel. The angel of God led Joseph to Egypt and then back to Israel at the appointed time. The guidance came through an angel both times.

We find in **Acts 10:30-32** the story of Cornelius. He said, "A MAN STOOD BEFORE ME." We discovered in the last chapter that many times angels appear as men. Cornelius said, "A MAN STOOD BEFORE ME . . . AND SAID . . . SEND TO JOPPA AND CALL SIMON, WHOSE SURNAME IS PETER, AND HE SHALL SPEAK UNTO THEE." Cornelius was crying out for God, and the angel appeared to him and told him to go get Peter. God has chosen men to preach the gospel, but He can surely use an angel to get someone for you to preach it to.

Then we find Gideon, in **Judges 6:12-15.** The angel of God came unto him and said, "Gideon, thou mighty man of valour, I am going to use you to defeat the Midianites." Gideon received guidance as to how to conquer the mighty enemy.

Joshua 5:14-15. Joshua went to look over the city of Jericho, and while he was looking Jericho over he said, "How am I going to take this huge city?" And all at once he saw a man standing there (a mighty man), and Joshua said, "Whose side are you on?" And he told him, "I am the leader of the host of the Lord's army." He came to give Joshua guidance. And angels will still give you and me guidance today.

VI. **REVELATIONS.** Angels bring revelations. The angel of God came to Zacharias and said, "Zacharias, Elisabeth is going to have a son, and you name him John." And you know what Zacharias did? He doubted, and said, "Well, how can I really know this is so?" And the angel of

30

God said, "You will not speak until he's born." Zacharias was in the temple burning incense, and the people were waiting for Zacharias to come outside, but he was a long time coming out. When Zacharias came out he couldn't talk, and for nine months Zacharias couldn't speak. Finally, the day the baby was to be named, everybody wanted to name him Zach, Jr. They asked Zacharias what the boy's name would be, and he took a table and "WROTE SAYING, HIS NAME IS JOHN . . . AND HIS MOUTH WAS OPENED IMMEDIATELY" (Luke 1:59-64). The angel had revealed to Zacharias many months earlier the things concerning the ministry of his son John. Revelation concerning many things can still come today by angels.

We are all familiar with the revelation of the ministry of Jesus in **Luke 1:26-38.** Let's look at what the angel told Mary. **Verse 31:** "AND BEHOLD, THOU SHALT CONCEIVE IN THY WOMB, AND BRING FORTH A SON, AND SHALT CALL HIS NAME JESUS. HE SHALL BE GREAT, AND SHALL BE CALLED THE SON OF THE HIGHEST: AND THE LORD GOD SHALL GIVE UNTO HIM THE THRONE OF HIS FATHER DAVID: AND HE SHALL REIGN OVER THE HOUSE OF JACOB FOR EVER; AND OF HIS KINGDOM THERE SHALL BE NO END. THEN SAID MARY UNTO THE ANGEL, HOW SHALL THIS BE, SEEING I KNOW NOT A MAN? AND THE ANGEL ANSWERED AND SAID UNTO HER, THE HOLY GHOST (The Holy Spirit) SHALL COME UPON THEE, AND THE POWER OF THE HIGHEST SHALL OVERSHADOW THEE: THEREFORE ALSO THAT HOLY THING WHICH SHALL BE BORN OF THEE SHALL BE CALLED THE SON OF GOD. AND, BEHOLD, THY COUSIN ELISABETH, SHE HATH ALSO CONCEIVED A SON IN HER OLD AGE: AND THIS IS THE SIXTH MONTH

WITH HER, WHO WAS CALLED BARREN. FOR WITH GOD NOTHING SHALL BE IMPOSSIBLE. AND MARY SAID, BEHOLD THE HANDMAID OF THE LORD; BE IT UNTO ME ACCORDING TO THY WORD. AND THE ANGEL DEPARTED FROM HER." I believe the best teaching I've ever taught is when I taught (in the Great Women of Faith Series) concerning Mary. You talk about faith! That young Hebrew girl had faith. Because she knew it took a man, but God said, "You don't need one," and she said, "Be it unto me according to thy word." We need to take the Word of God like that today, too.

VII. **PROTECTION.** Let's observe a few Scriptures on protection. This is another way angels help God's people, and this is primarily what we are dealing with. In the next chapter we will start dealing with the conditions of protection. There are various conditions you must meet in order for God's angels to protect you, and we will consider those conditions in chapter three.

Psalm 34:7, "THE ANGEL OF THE LORD EN-CAMPETH ROUND ABOUT THEM THAT FEAR HIM, AND DELIVERETH THEM." God's angels are assigned to encamp around His people and to deliver them.

Psalm 91:11, "FOR HE SHALL GIVE HIS ANGELS CHARGE OVER THEE, TO KEEP THEE IN ALL THY WAYS."

Exodus 14:19-20 is another example. "THE ANGEL OF GOD, WHICH WENT BEFORE THE CAMP OF IS-RAEL, REMOVED AND WENT BEHIND THEM;" between the Israelites and the Egyptians. Here's what was going on: the Israelites were leaving, and Moses was out in front. And you know who was out in front of Moses? The Angel of God, which went before the camp of Israel. When they stopped by the Red Sea, and the Egyptians were closing in, we find the angel removed and went behind them, between the Israelites and the Egyptians. The angel provided the protection from the enemy.

II Kings 6:17 says Elisha was in the mountain. The king of Syria was trying to defeat Israel. Every time they would try to take Israel, they would make their plan and the Israelites would know the enemy's plan. The king of Syria came to the decision, and said, "Somebody in my inner circle is betraying me." And they said, "No, King; there's a prophet in Israel and he knows what you talk about in your sleep." He said, "We must kill that prophet; he's keeping us from winning this war." So he sent a great army, and they surrounded the Israelites. Elisha and his servant came out one morning and the servant looked out and said, "What's going on? Look at all that army!" Elisha came outside and said, "Don't be afraid; there are more for us than against us." Now can't you picture the servant looking out but he couldn't see anybody? and here's Elisha saying, "Don't worry, there are more for us than against us." Elisha had eyes that could see into the invisible, eyes that could see the things of God. The Scripture says Elisha prayed and said, "God, open his eyes," and about that time the servant's eyes were opened, and it says the mountain was full of horses and chariots of fire round about Elisha. If God would open our eyes, we would see angels protecting us all the time. I believe the angels are smiling as you read, because they are saying, "Look there, they are studying about our work and our ministry. They are beginning to believe in us and give us opportunity to fulfill what we were made for." The angels were created by God, and they have a ministry, but they need Christians to believe in them so they can fulfill their ministry.

Following is a list of Scriptures concerning Divine Protection.

Psalm 34:7, "THE ANGEL OF THE LORD ENCAMPETH ROUND ABOUT THEM THAT FEAR HIM, AND DELIVERETH THEM."

Psalm 84:11, "FOR THE LORD GOD IS A SUN (He will lighten your pathway) AND SHIELD: THE LORD WILL GIVE GRACE AND GLORY: NO GOOD THING WILL HE WITHHOLD FROM THEM THAT WALK UPRIGHTLY."

Psalm 91:10,11,12, "THERE SHALL NO EVIL BEFALL THEE, NEITHER SHALL ANY PLAGUE COME NIGH THEY DWELLING. FOR HE SHALL GIVE HIS ANGELS CHARGE OVER THEE, TO KEEP THEE IN **ALL** THY WAYS. THEY SHALL BEAR **THEE** UP IN **THEIR** HANDS, LEST THOU DASH THY FOOT AGAINST A STONE."

Psalm 115:11, "YE THAT FEAR THE LORD (or reverence the Lord), TRUST IN THE LORD: HE IS THEIR HELP AND THEIR SHIELD." He is their protection. How is God your shield and your protection? Because you believe that His angels encamp round about you because you belong to the Lord.

Psalm 121:7, "THE LORD SHALL PRESERVE THEE FROM ALL EVIL." **How** will He preserve me from all evil? By my trusting His Word and believing that His angels encamp round about me. He will use them, because Hebrews 1:14 says ministering angels are sent forth to minister to the heirs of salvation, and that's all who have accepted Jesus Christ as Lord and Saviour.

Proverbs 2:8, "HE KEEPETH THE PATHS OF JUDGMENT, AND PRESERVETH THE WAY OF HIS SAINTS."

Proverbs 2:10-12, "WHEN WISDOM ENTERETH INTO THINE HEART, AND KNOWLEDGE IS PLEASANT UNTO THY SOUL; DISCRETION SHALL PRESERVE THEE, UNDERSTANDING SHALL KEEP THEE (what understanding? understanding about God's angels): TO DELIVER THEE FROM THE WAY OF THE EVIL MAN, FROM THE MAN THAT SPEAKETH FRO-

WARD THINGS'' (who speaks things that would cause you troubles and problems). So he says, "TO DELIVER THEE FROM THE WAY OF THE EVIL MAN." Do you need that?

Proverbs 11:8, "THE RIGHTEOUS IS DELIVERED OUT OF TROUBLE, AND THE WICKED COMETH IN HIS STEAD." The righteous — we are the righteousness of God in Christ. That means **we** are delivered out of trouble.

Proverbs 14:3, ". . . THE LIPS OF THE WISE SHALL PRESERVE THEM." How will the lips of the wise preserve them? The Bible says you can have what you say (Mark 11:23,24). I say, "The angels of the Lord encamp round about me," because Psalm 34:7 says they do. Now that's "wise lips." You know what wise lips are? Lips that say what God says. God says His angels encamp round about us; therefore, the lips of the wise shall preserve them. That means your wise lips shall protect you, and keep you because you confess that God's angels do encamp round about you.

Proverbs 30:5, "EVERY WORD OF GOD IS PURE: HE IS A SHIELD UNTO THEM THAT PUT THEIR TRUST IN HIM." How does He shield you? With His angels; that's their ministry. The enemy attacks, but the angels of the Lord guard you, as a shield.

Luke 10:19, "BEHOLD, I GIVE UNTO YOU POWER TO TREAD UPON SERPENTS (the devil) AND SCORPIONS (demons), AND OVER ALL THE POWER OF THE ENEMY: AND **NOTHING** SHALL BY ANY MEANS HURT YOU." — **"Nothing** shall by any means hurt you."

John 17:15,16, This is the prayer of Jesus, and this is what He says: "I PRAY NOT THAT THOU SHOULDEST TAKE THEM OUT OF THE WORLD, BUT THAT THOU SHOULDEST KEEP THEM FROM THE EVIL." Do you believe that prayer was answered? Let me tell you what Jesus prayed: He said, "I pray **not** that thou shouldest take them out of the world; I'm not praying that You will take them out of all this stuff; but that thou shouldest keep them from evil." "THEY ARE NOT OF THE WORLD, EVEN AS I AM NOT OF THE WORLD." We are born of God; we are of another world; we're just passing through this one, but we can have God's protection as we pass through.

II Thessalonians 3:2,3, "AND THAT WE MAY BE DELIVERED FROM UNREASONABLE AND WICKED MEN: FOR ALL MEN HAVE NOT FAITH. BUT THE LORD IS FAITHFUL, WHO SHALL STABLISH YOU, AND KEEP YOU FROM EVIL." Do you know God is going to establish the Christian? He is establishing us by faith in the Word of God, to believe in the power of His angels to keep us from evil. "BUT THE LORD IS FAITHFUL, WHO SHALL STABLISH YOU, AND KEEP YOU FROM EVIL." Would you like to be kept from evil?

II Timothy 4:17,18, "NOTWITHSTANDING THE LORD STOOD WITH ME, AND STRENGTHENED ME; THAT BY ME THE PREACHING MIGHT BE FULLY KNOWN . . . I WAS DELIVERED OUT OF THE MOUTH OF THE LION. AND THE LORD SHALL DELIVER ME FROM EVERY EVIL WORK, AND WILL PRESERVE ME UNTO HIS HEAVENLY KINGDOM." Daniel wasn't the only one delivered from lions. Paul said, "I was delivered **out** of the mouth of the lion." Who closed those lions' mouths for Daniel? An angel? Is that protection? They threw Daniel into the lions' den and the angel of the Lord closed the lions' mouths to protect him. The Bible is filled with examples of God's protection. "AND THE LORD SHALL DELIVER ME FROM **EVERY** EVIL WORK (that's good news), AND WILL PRESERVE ME UNTO HIS HEAVENLY KINGDOM."

Here are some Scriptures on long life.

Psalm 90:10, "THE DAYS OF OUR YEARS ARE THREESCORE YEARS AND TEN (that's 70); AND IF BY REASON OF STRENGTH THEY BE FOURSCORE YEARS (80)." Here's how I confess it: "The days of my life are a minimum of 70, unless Jesus comes to get me, and if by reason of strength (and I'm strong and healthy) they will be fourscore (80); and if Jesus hasn't come to get me that strength will get me 100 years." You may say, "Brother Willis, I don't believe it." Well, you go ahead and die young, die early and die sick, die miserable! I'm sold on God's angels to protect me.

Proverbs 3:1,2, "MY SON, FORGET NOT MY LAW; BUT LET THINE HEART KEEP MY COMMAND-MENTS: FOR LENGTH OF DAYS, AND LONG LIFE, AND PEACE, SHALL THEY ADD TO THEE." This is a good promise.

Proverbs 4:10, "HEAR, O MY SON, AND RECEIVE (in other words, Hear, O my son, and believe) MY SAY-INGS; AND THE YEARS OF THY LIFE SHALL BE MANY." It doesn't say a few, it says many. This word "shall" means it's mandatory, a must. If you will receive His Word (He says receive my sayings, receive God's Word), then it is mandatory that the years of your life be many. Anybody interested?

Proverbs 9:11, "FOR BY ME (God) THY DAYS SHALL BE MULTIPLIED, AND THE YEARS OF THY LIFE SHALL BE INCREASED." "By Me."

Proverbs 1:27, "THE FEAR OF THE LORD PRO-LONGETH DAYS." A reverence of the Lord and His Word, believing in God's angels, will prolong your days.

If you are interested in God's protection, make this confession: "In the name of Jesus I believe God's Word. And God's Word says that the angels of the Lord encamp round about me. I believe they encamp round about me and my family, and our possessions and property. I confess that no evil shall befall me, my family, our possessions or property, because I abide under the shadow of the Almighty God, and God alone is my refuge and my fortress. In God alone do I trust. God's Word is my shield and my armour. God's angels have been sent forth by Him to protect those who are the heirs of salvation; to protect those who are born of God, and I am born of God. Therefore, God has many angels to send forth to protect those who believe in Him and His angels. And I'm a believer, not a doubter; and because I believe, I shall receive. I will not doubt and do without. I do believe, and I therefore receive. Amen.''

Saints, stand for God's angels to protect you, your husband, your wife, your sons and your daughters; to protect you as you travel, protect you as you walk, protect you in everything you do. They will stay with you on the job, men. Ladies, they are with you at home. Children, they are with you at school. They are there to take care of you. It doesn't make any difference where you are. If you go on vacation, they will go with you. I confess God's protection all the time; why don't you begin to do the same, today?

CHAPTER THREE
CONDITIONS FOR ANGEL PROTECTION

OUTLINE

I. **COMPUTER REPROGRAMMING**

II. **CONSTANT CONTACT:**
1. "Dwelleth" - abide, settled, lodges securely and quietly.
2. "Secret place" - hiding place; "shall abide" - continuous.
3. "Shadow" - implies nearness, close companion.
4. "Under his wings" - young bird to mother.

III. **CONTINUOUS CONFESSION:**
1. Psalm 91:2, "I WILL SAY":
  A. "My refuge" - escape from danger - retreat from.
  B. "My fortress" - stronghold - tower of defense.
  C. "My God" - all the time - all situations.
  D. "In him will I trust." - Hebrew, "him alone."
2. Isaiah 54:17, "No weapon that is formed against thee shall prosper."

3. Proverbs 14:3, "The lips of the wise shall preserve them."

IV. CONFIDENCE IN THE WORD: 91:4, "His truth shall be thy shield and buckler."

1. Psalm 112:7, "He shall not be afraid of evil tidings: his heart is fixed, trusting in the Lord."
2. Psalm 121:7, "The Lord shall preserve thee from all evil: he shall preserve thy soul" (mind, will, emotions).

V. COMPLETE LOVE: 91:14, "Because he hath set his love upon me":

1. I John 4:18, "Perfect love casteth out fear . . . He that feareth is not made perfect in love."
2. Luke 14:26, "If any man come to me and hate not his father, and mother, and wife, and children, and brethren, and sisters . . . and his own life also, he cannot be my disciple."

VI. COMPREHEND THE POWER OF HIS NAME

CHAPTER THREE
CONDITIONS FOR ANGEL PROTECTION

INTRODUCTION: In this chapter we are going to deal with conditions for angel protection. We will be primarily studying in Psalm 91, but let us observe one Scripture from **Hebrews 11, verse 6**: "BUT WITHOUT FAITH IT IS IMPOSSIBLE TO PLEASE HIM: FOR HE THAT COMETH TO GOD MUST BELIEVE THAT HE IS, AND THAT HE IS A REWARDER OF THEM THAT DILIGENTLY SEEK HIM." There is no way God's angels can consistently protect you unless you believe in them. This is the reason for this study guide, to help give you a Scriptural foundation so you can exercise faith in God's angels. Faith can never operate beyond your knowledge of the Word of God. We considered in the first chapter the fact that angels have two primary functions. Their first function is they are messengers of God. They deliver God's message, and we observed many examples of their delivering messages to God's people. In the second area we noticed their function is to protect God's people.

As Christians learn the Word of God, and begin to

41

exercise faith in the Scriptures that talk about protection by angels, the angels will encamp round about, and build a shield about their families and protect them from the evil that is in the world, and the even greater evil that is coming upon this world. Our purpose in this chapter is to consider conditions for angel protection. Let's look at these conditions.

I. **COMPUTER REPROGRAMMING**: The very first condition we will talk about is that every individual must have his computer (mind) reprogrammed. Simply, your mind must be renewed by the Word of God. Most people, when you talk about angels, will say, "Folklore, myth, fairy tale, fantasy." They think of a little baby angel with rosy cheeks, playing a harp. If that's the concept you have of angels, no wonder they couldn't protect you. We observe in the Bible that one angel was powerful enough to kill 185,000 men. That's no baby playing a harp! They are creations of God, and there are hosts of powerful angels. Jesus could have called 10,000 angels to deliver Him from the Cross. Your mind must be reprogrammed.

Romans 12:2, "BE NOT CONFORMED TO THIS WORLD . . . " What does this world think about angels? They think you are crazy; they think you are some kind of religious nut, a fanatic, going off the deep end, if you believe in angels. Paul says, "BE NOT CONFORMED TO THIS WORLD." He is saying, "Don't think like this world; because as long as you think like this world you will receive what they receive." The world has taught you to think their way, but God says, " . . . BUT BE YE TRANS-FORMED BY THE RENEWING OF YOUR MIND" (the re-wiring, the renovating, by taking the Word of God and planting it in your mind.) For years our minds have been programmed by the garbage of the world, part of which says, "no angels." What does the world say about laying hands on the sick? They say, "No, go to the doctor." Well, that's the world's concept; that's the heathens' concept. But you're not heathens any longer. Or are you? If you are born again you are not a heathen any more. What is a heathen, Brother Willis? It's any man or woman who doesn't have Jesus Christ as his personal saviour. They're heathens (the Greek bears this out). So if you don't have Jesus Christ as your personal saviour, you're a heathen. Now I didn't say you were, God said you were. If you want to argue, argue with Him. A heathen is someone who has another god. If you haven't been born of God, then you have another god. It may be your self; it may be your own intellectual ability. It could be anything; but if it's not Jesus Christ, then you are heathen and worship another god. **Romans 12:2** says, "BE YE TRANSFORMED BY THE RENEWING OF YOUR MIND, THAT YE MAY PROVE WHAT IS THAT GOOD, AND ACCEPTABLE, AND PERFECT, WILL OF GOD." Not the perfect will of **man**; we don't need anyone to teach us the ways of man. We know the ways of man, and the ways of man have nothing to do with angels. Therefore, if you are going to meet the conditions for angel protection, you must get your mind renewed. That's why I have given you the Scriptures about protection; because you need to start meditating those Scriptures until they become real to you. (A study guide on the "Conquest of the Mind" is available from Fill The Gap. It is a detailed study guide concerning renewing your mind.)

Here's another Scripture: **Psalm 1:1**, "BLESSED IS THE MAN THAT WALKETH NOT IN THE COUNSEL OF THE UNGODLY." Simply, it means this: Blessed is the man that does not listen to the advice of the lost man. What do the ungodly tell you about angels? God says: Blessed is the man that doesn't walk according to, nor listen to, the counsel of the heathen. What do they tell you about healing? They tell you to go to a doctor; the Bible tells you to go to God. They tell you if you want money to go to the bank; God tells you to come to Him. They tell you to get Blue Cross, not the Old Rugged Cross. They tell you to get a piece of rock, when you have THE ROCK. Why settle for a **piece** of the rock, when you have **the** Rock, Jesus Christ, the Son of God? Really, it's ridiculous for a Christian to trust in man. You have God to trust in, and you let somebody sell you on something else. And this is what He says: "BLESSED IS THE MAN THAT WALKETH NOT IN THE COUNSEL OF THE UNGODLY" (doesn't listen to the counsel and the advice of the ungodly). The ungodly man can't tell you anything that has to do with God. He may be the smartest man in the world, but he can be spiritually ignorant. If he doesn't know Jesus, he is spiritually ignorant. He's illiterate as far as the things of God are concerned. But he could be a big businessman out in the world and still die and go to hell, lose it all, and accomplish nothing. That is what the Bible says (read Luke 12:16-32).

Here's another Scripture to help you realize your computer, your mind, must be reprogrammed, renewed by the Word of God. **Proverbs 3:5**, "TRUST IN" Blue Cross, and Blue Shield, and Prudential, and security, and insurance. **NO**, it says, "TRUST IN **THE LORD**." But, Brother Willis, I think we ought to trust in those earthly things. Show me the Scripture that says trust in insurance. That's the recommendation of the world; it's not from the Bible. My Bible says, "TRUST IN THE LORD." It doesn't say man's systems; it says, "TRUST IN THE LORD WITH (how much of thine heart?) **ALL** THINE HEART: AND LEAN NOT UNTO THINE OWN UNDERSTANDING." What do most people do? They lean to their own understanding, therefore, they have Blue Cross. They lean to their own understanding, and they are trusting a man to heal them, when the power of God is available to heal them *every* time they are sick. Your mind must be renewed to God's kind of thinking, the Bible kind of thinking. If you don't know the Bible, the things we are considering will blow your mind. That's why your computer has to be reprogrammed. You must get rid of that 10 watt fuse and put in a 20 watt fuse, because the Bible just won't line up with what we have been taught for many years. The Bible didn't come from a man; it came from God.

The first thing to do is realize you are not to be conformed to this world, and what the world says about angels. God says, "BLESSED IS THE MAN THAT WALKETH NOT IN THE COUNSEL OF THE UNGODLY." What do the ungodly say about angels? God says, "TRUST IN THE LORD WITH ALL THINE HEART; AND LEAN NOT UNTO THINE OWN UNDERSTANDING." What does your own understanding say about angels? Figment of the imagination, folklore! Here are three Scriptures, saints; and the Bible says let it be confirmed in the mouth of two or three witnesses. Here are three Scriptures that tell you that if you are going to walk in divine protection you are going to have to get your mind renewed by the Word of God.

II. **CONSTANT CONTACT WITH GOD:** A second condition is that you must have constant contact with God. **Psalm 91:1**, "HE THAT DWELLETH IN THE SECRET PLACE OF THE MOST HIGH **SHALL ABIDE UNDER THE SHADOW** OF THE ALMIGHTY (God)."

1. "**Dwelleth**" means "abide, settled, to lodge securely and quietly." This means you must have constant contact with God, dwelling in that secret, sacred place.

2. "Secret place." The secret place is a hiding place. It says you shall abide **under** the shadow of the Almighty God; that means continuously. He means continually you must stay in that secret place, that hiding place, close to God. Settle down there close to God, and He will keep you safe.

45

3. "Shadow." If you abide, and stay under the shadow of the Almighty God; and the word "shadow" implies nearness, doesn't it? Think about being in someone's shadow. Even if it's late in the afternoon, the shadow won't go but so far, so it implies nearness, a close companionship.

4. "Under his wings" - **Psalm 91:4** says "UNDER HIS WINGS" shall we abide. This is like a young bird and a mother, a young chick and a mother hen. You know young chicks can be all scattered out in the barnyard, and somebody will make a lot of noise, and that old mama hen will cluck, cluck, cluck and raise her wings, and those chicks head for safety, under mother's wings. That's where you and I are supposed to abide; God is just like the mother hen. We need to be close to Him all the time. But you know if a little chick gets away from the mama chicken, too far, a snake may get it, or a rat may get it. God tells you and me that we are to dwell in the secret place, under His wings, and no evil will befall us. It implies having a constant contact with God. If you are going to believe in protection by God's angels, you must be willing to line up your life with God and say, "God, I'm going to stay near you." It is only as you abide under that shadow of the Almighty God and stay in constant contact and constant relationship with Him, that it will work continually. Remember, there must be constant contact with your heavenly Father.

III. **CONTINUOUS CONFESSION**: Thirdly, there must be continuous confession, if God's angels are going to move on your behalf and protect you consistently.

1. **Psalm 91:2**, "**I WILL SAY** OF THE LORD, HE IS MY REFUGE AND MY FORTRESS: MY GOD; IN HIM WILL I TRUST." Who is going to say this? **You** must confess it; **you** must come to the place you are bold enough in the Lord, based upon the Word of God, to say:

46

A. **"God is my refuge;** He is my escape from danger; He is the One Who is my refuge and fortress." You must say it with your mouth. **Job 22:28** says, "THOU SHALT . . . DECREE A THING AND IT SHALL BE ESTABLISHED UNTO YOU." **Mark 11:23** says you can have whatsoever you say. But you are going to have to say it. I will say, "God is my refuge; He is my escape from danger."

B. "**God is my fortress**; He is my stronghold; He is my tower of defense." Run to God, to defend you. "I WILL SAY . . . HE IS MY GOD"; all the time in all situations, not just sometimes. Verse 2, "IN HIM WILL I TRUST." The Hebrew means "in Him alone." It doesn't mean God plus Blue Cross; it doesn't mean God plus your securities. "I believe in God's angels, but I'm going to keep man's way, too." If you do, you will be limited, because the Bible says, "I will say, **God** is my refuge; **God** is my fortress."

C. "**MY GOD**." How often is He your God? Is He your God all the time? Or is He just really your God until you get in trouble? How far is He really your God? "Oh, Brother Willis, I believe He can save me from the grave" — but yet He can't protect you? Really, that is a contradiction, to believe that God has that power, and then not trust Him fully.

D. "**IN HIM WILL I TRUST**." In whom are you trusting? Who are you trusting to take you to heaven? Is it God plus anything else? Well, brothers and sisters, as you live in this life it doesn't have to be God plus anything else, either. If you want the protection of God, He doesn't believe in your trying to be double-insured. He doesn't want you two-timing Him. He doesn't want you to say, "Oh, God, I believe in You," but yet you have an ace-in-the-hole behind His back. "Oh, God, I'm trusting You; I believe Your angels encamp all around about me." "Well, what is it you have back there?" "What are you talking about,

God? That's just my burial policy I've had for 30 years."
"What's that for?" "Well, You know how it is, God." No,
He doesn't know how it is. What are you trusting in? Be
honest before the Lord.

2. **Isaiah 54:17** says, "NO WEAPON THAT IS
FORMED AGAINST THEE SHALL PROSPER." When
you are trusting God and His angels, He says no weapon
that is formed against you shall prosper. You need to read
all of that Scripture in Isaiah 54:17.

3. **Proverbs 14:3** says, "THE LIPS OF THE WISE
SHALL PRESERVE THEM." Do you know what most
Christians are trusting in today to preserve them? Insurance. Saints, insurance only offers you help **after** something happens; angels **keep it from happening**. The
world's insurance system is a good one; they've gotten
filthy rich from man's fears. That's all they do — teach you
fear. Not long ago, they were advertising traveler's checks
on TV; and they showed a family going on vacation, and
they lost their money. There they were, discouraged; then
the voice said, "Now, if you had purchased traveler's
checks that wouldn't have happened to you." Fear! They
show a picture of a woman walking on the seashore, then
show her cleaning the closets out, with her face real, real
long; and she says, "I never thought it would happen to
John." Then the insurance company advertisement says,
"Protect yourself from these things." **Anything that operates on the basis of fear is not of God**, because God
says, "I haven't given you a spirit of fear, but of power, and
love, and a sound mind" (II Timothy 1:7). The only way
they can sell anything is to work on man's fears, work on
man's insecurities and inferiorities. Some of you, as you
read this, will know what I'm talking about. You may sell
insurance; if you do, you know what I'm talking about.
Some of you have sold it in the past, so you know this is
how it operates.

48

The Psalmist David says, "I WILL SAY OF THE LORD, HE IS MY REFUGE AND MY FORTRESS: MY GOD; IN HIM (alone) WILL I TRUST." I confess it every day: "Praise God, God alone is my refuge; and God is my fortress; in Him alone do I trust." This is not a popular message, because you know 99% of all families have insurance. A lot of people are getting rich from it, so it's not a popular message when you say, Don't have it. I've had some big insurance executives and agencies, in the city I pastor, call me up: "Rev. Willis, this is So-and-So of So-and-So agency. I've had someone recently cancel their insurance and I wanted to get some things straight. I just wanted to call and check with you about it. Is it true that you preach against insurance?" I would say, "It's simply this — believe in insurance or believe in God. Are you trying to tell me I ought to tell the people to trust you more than God?" The insurance man would say, "Aw, well, we need to be logical about it." I said, "No, when I was logical you could get rich because of me. I was all right when I was logical and reasonable; as long as you were making money. But now that I'm not logical and reasonable, I'm no good any more?" He would then say, "Aw, well, I'll talk to you later." If you don't believe me, you just tell your agent you're going to cancel yours and see how much he loves you. If you think you're so precious, such a good friend to them, you're going to see how much a friend you are, because they're going to try to sell you on keeping it; to help you out. **They work on your fear**. Praise God, His angels will take care of you. I realize this is a big step, because we've been programmed all of our life to go man's way. When I was born my Daddy took out a policy on me. You know, that was the smart thing to do; if you really love your children, the first thing you do is take out an educational insurance policy on them. You plan for their future; plan for their college. The figures prove that a small percentage of them ever go to college.

"I WILL SAY OF THE LORD, HE IS MY REFUGE AND MY FORTRESS." I can remember when this Scripture became real to me. I was lying on the floor in the parsonage of the First Baptist Church in Baldwin, Louisiana. I was seeking God concerning some things, and God spoke to me and said, "Son, do you believe in divine healing?" I said, "That's right." He said, "I want to ask you something, son. What do you have your insurance policies for?" I lay there on the floor and I thought for a moment, **"Just in case."** Ace in the hole! That's what I thought — just in case, you know, just in **case** I had a wreck. The insurance principle is based on . . . just in case. I **sold** insurance a long time ago; I believed in it. I thought since I really loved my wife, I had plenty of insurance, just in case I died early she and the children would have plenty. And that's why most men are **dying** early today — because that's their confession. "Now, Honey, I want you to know right here in this box are all my insurance policies. If I go before you, here's what you do," and you know that men are dying nine to one earlier than women because that's what they believe in and have confessed upon themselves for years? My wife doesn't feel that way about me; she's praying, "God, You keep that man alive." She goes around saying, "Father, I thank You he is strong and healthy and he's going to live long, long, long, and be prosperous." Listen to me, God showed this to me: most men are committing suicide with their confessions, and guaranteeing they are going to die before their wives. And most of the wives are helping them, and they think they are doing the right thing. And I'll tell you what: go check with the insurance companies; the death charts prove it. The figures prove that the men are going first. You may say it is because you work hard. No, it's because you have a bad mouth. You are not saying, "God is my refuge"; you are

50

not saying, "God is my strength." You are not saying, "The angels of the Lord encamp round about me." You are not saying, "God promised me 70 years at least." You may say, "Well, I'm just going to get by as long as I can, and when it's my time I'll go on home." I'm going to get by as long as **I** can, too — at least 70; then I'll be ready to go on home. I'm not in any hurry, I'm enjoying it down here. With Jesus it's good. It's going to be better up there; but I want to live to see God manifest Himself more before I go home.

IV. **CONFIDENCE IN THE WORD:** Here is another condition for protection by angels: confidence in the Word. **Psalm 91:4** says, "HIS TRUTH SHALL BE THY SHIELD AND BUCKLER." The Word "buckler" means "armor."

1. **Psalm 112:7,** "HE SHALL NOT BE AFRAID OF EVIL TIDINGS." Do you know that most people live in fear of evil tidings? If their children are a little bit late coming in from school, what do they start thinking about? If the husband is a few hours late; or, many wives go grocery shopping at night and are supposed to be back at 7 o'clock, and it's 8:30 — what does the devil start trying to put in the husband's mind? Many times the devil causes children to have fear when mother and dad are gone, telling them something is going to happen to mom and dad. The devil attacked one of my daughters, because of my traveling so much. The devil would tell her, "He isn't going to come back; he's gone this time and he'll never be back again." Psalm 112:7 says, "HE SHALL **NOT** BE AFRAID OF EVIL TIDINGS: HIS HEART IS FIXED, TRUSTING IN THE LORD." Those who trust in God shall not be afraid of evil tidings, because his truth shall be their shield and buckler.

2. Psalm 121:7, "THE LORD SHALL PRESERVE THEE FROM ALL EVIL: HE SHALL PRESERVE THY

SOUL." Your soul is your **mind**, your **will**, and your **emotions**. If you keep your eyes on God and learn to trust Him, His Word will preserve you — your mind, your will, and your emotions. But you will have to be trusting in God. You must have confidence in the Word of God. Listen to me carefully: **You always go to the one you have the most confidence in.** I'm going to tell you what you're using today: **what you believe in the most.** When you get sick, who are you going to go to? The one you believe can help you the most. When you need money, who will you go to? The one you believe can help you the most. When you're thinking about protection, I'll tell you what you are going to do — you are going to go to the one you think you can trust the most. It is easy for you to find out if you trust in God more than man. "Brother Willis, are you telling me to get rid of all my insurance?" No, I'm not; not until you get the protection Word in your heart. I'm just giving you enough Scripture so you can begin to do it. Don't do it just because I'm doing it; learn the Word of God. We have lived since 1971 without any kind of insurance — none at all. No hospitalization, no medical, no life, no retirement; no car insurance, no home insurance, nothing. "Brother Willis, have you ever lost anything?" Bought a 1977 Cadillac — drove it five miles, and totalled it out. "What did you do when you bought the next one?" I had my angels on it. The devil tried to cause fear in me to stop me. And that's what he tries to do with you. When I first started to come into God's protection, in 1971, I cancelled all the insurance I could; I still owed on my car, so I couldn't cancel it. I was confessing the angels of the Lord encamp round about me, and no evil should befall me. I drove to Beaumont, Texas to speak at a Full Gospel Business Men's meeting. I was driving back early Sunday morning to get back in time to minister in the Sunday morning service in the church I was pastoring at

52

the time. I got about 20 miles outside of Beaumont and it began sprinkling rain. For no justifiable reason at all (I was not speeding, I was wide awake), all at once my car went into a spin. When it did I knew it was the devil; I just knew it, and I said, "I **rebuke** you, Satan, in the Name of Jesus." I just began to say, "Jesus!" That was about all I had time to say; sometimes that's all you have time to say, so you have to have the assurance down inside of you. Amen? It's time you realized the devil is out to kill you; your sons, your daughters, your husband, your wife, your mother, your daddy, your brothers, your sisters, your friends. He's a killer! John 10:10 says Jesus came that you might have life, and that more abundantly. The devil has come to steal, kill, and destroy. You need to realize that he hates Christians more than anybody in the whole world. He's out to kill you! Therefore, you need to learn how to exercise faith for protection.

The reason I taught this series and put it into a study guide is because God said, "Son, tough days are coming. My people don't know how to believe Me for protection, and they are going to be bombarded by all kinds of troubles." When things get rough and riots are going on and troubles and problems, there will be break-ins and everything else, and then what are you going to do? — get a gun and shoot them? When the Bible says, "Thou shalt not kill!" "Oh, but, Brother Willis, I have a right to protect my property." Give me the Scripture that says you can kill to protect it. "Well, if someone grabbed my little daughter, I'd kill them." You probably would, and disobey the Word of God which says, "Thou shalt not kill." I know what you think — you think it's all right, but it's never justifiable. I don't care if they take three of your daughters and your wife and rape them right in front of you, you don't have a right to kill them. That's the Word of God. Now the flesh doesn't like that. I understand now; I'm not being mean nor cruel. I'm just trying to help you to face some things.

Because I love and appreciate God's children, I am telling them the truth. You need to learn the Word of God about protection, then let God's angels protect your family, and you will NEVER have to worry about robbers and rapists. There is only one sure way to protect your family, by faith in God's Word that His angels will take care of your family. You are foolish if you're trusting anything else — you are unwise. Even if you're just three blocks away, you can't do them any good. You can only get there and help after something has happened. On the other hand, you can have faith in God and the angels can be right there all the time. Mama, those kids at school, that son working 200 miles from home, that daughter 300 miles from home; you have only one thing that can really work — trust in God and His Word. Saints, you need to see this thing and see it clearly, that you must have confidence in the Word of God for protection.

It costs to learn the Word so you can move into these things. Don't jump out on it too quickly; keep your insurance if you have it, until the Word begins to work inside of you and you can't keep it any more. Let me just give you a good example. I can't kill. "Thou shalt not kill." It's just as strong inside of me not to have insurance — "Thou shalt not have insurance," as it is "Thou shalt not kill." But, you see, I've got so much of the Word in me on this thing; but you can't do that until you get the Word of God in you, too. "So what do I do, Brother Willis?" Keep your insurance; but start getting these Scriptures and meditating on them and thinking on them and say, "Hey, God, I want the best policy there is in the world. God, I want to get the best protection there is for me and my family, and our possessions and our property. I want the best. And, God, since You are the best and the most powerful, then what You have to offer must be the best. But, Lord, I didn't know about Your way; I've always used man because I didn't know there was a better way. But now, God, I'm going to search the Scriptures; and I'm going to find the better way." Then you will get to the place where you "shall **not** be afraid of evil tidings," and trust the Lord for the total protection of your loved ones.

V. **COMPLETE LOVE. Psalm 91:14,** "BECAUSE HE HAS SET HIS LOVE UPON ME . . ." As you read Psalm 91, when you come to the 11th or 12th verse it changes and God is speaking. This is how you should read it: "Because I have set **my** love upon **Him,** therefore **He** will deliver me. He will set me on high because I have known His name. I shall call upon Him, and He will answer me; He will be with me in trouble; He will deliver me, and honour me. With long life will He satisfy me, and show me His salvation." That's how to read it, in the first person. So I say, "Because I have set my love upon Him, therefore will He deliver me."

1. **I John 4:18** says, "PERFECT LOVE CASTETH OUT FEAR . . . HE THAT FEARETH IS NOT MADE PERFECT IN LOVE." So one of the conditions is that if you really love God, then you are going to trust Him. God's Word says the angels of the Lord encamp round about you, and no evil shall befall you (Psalm 34:7).

2. **Luke 14:26,** "IF ANY MAN (or any person) COME TO ME (as you and I), AND HATE NOT HIS FATHER (in other words, the choice between going with them or going with God — you hate that choice), AND MOTHER, AND WIFE (or husband), AND CHILDREN, AND BRETH-REN, AND SISTERS, YEA, AND HIS OWN LIFE ALSO, HE CANNOT BE MY DISCIPLE." That is love. If any man come to Me and hate not his father, mother, wife, children, brothers and sisters, and his own life, he cannot be My disciple. Are you sure you want to be a disciple of the Lord Jesus Christ? "You mean, Brother Willis, I have

to put God first? **Yes**. It's through our love for God that He will really do these things in our lives. There must be a complete love. But if you don't really love Him, then you don't really trust Him. You can tell me you love God, but the only way you can prove it is by your trust. You can tell me all day, "I love God." You can sing, "Oh, how I love Jesus," for fifty years. How do you prove you love somebody? You trust them, but you have to prove it, don't you? You know how you prove you love God? By trusting Him, by putting Him first in your life, by saying, "God, You are number one in my life; God, You are my refuge; God, You are my fortress; God, in You alone do I trust." The conditions must be met. More and more, people are reaching out to divine protection. Most places I go and start talking about the Old Rugged Cross before Blue Cross, it blows their minds. They've heard some, but they haven't heard about this aspect of it. You must come to the place you love God and say, "Lord, I trust You with my complete life. I put my life in Your hands. God, if **You** can't take care of me, how can anyone else do it?" If God can't take care of your wife, or your husband, or your children, how in the world can you? How foolish it is for people to think they can do something that God can't do. But when we realize that God can do these things, we'll come into a new plateau in our walk with God. So one condition is complete love, which leads to complete trust.

VI. **COMPREHEND THE POWER OF HIS NAME.**
Another condition is that you must comprehend the power of God's name. **Psalm 91:14,** ". . . BECAUSE HE HATH KNOWN **MY NAME**," not knowing **about** Him, which does not last long or changes; but a personal relationship that develops continuously. You must know the power in the Name of Jesus, the Son of God. The only way you can know that is by continuously studying and learning the Word of God. "BECAUSE HE HATH **KNOWN**

56

MY NAME," not knowing **about** His Name. Many people know about God; many people say, "I know God is able to do anything." That's good, but the devil knows that much. If you just know He is able, you don't know any more than the devil knows. If you're just saying, "I believe God is able to protect me," the devil knows that. You're in the same boat with the devil. Until you go further, you will have to do something to prove it. The Bible says the demons believe, and tremble. What do they believe? They believe everything God says is true. But they are not saved (neither is Satan), and won't be. You can say, "Brother Willis, I believe God is able to do anything." Prove it! "Oh, but Brother Willis, it may cost me" — that's right. What most people have is a walkie-talkie Christianity. They walk and talk, but have no willingness to produce; not willing to put their lives on the line. We like a shouting message, as long as it doesn't cost anything. And when you start talking about protection by angels (or anything else), it will require diligence to study the Word of God. If you pay half the premium, don't expect much. If you trust Him halfway, don't expect much. You have to pay the whole premium in order to get all the benefits of the policy. You have to pay the full price in order to get all the benefits of the policy. So many Christians think they can take half of it and get half benefit. God's grace will bless you, but it's just grace; it's not because you're trusting Him or not because you're loving Him. You haven't really come to the place you are really trusting God unless you really put your life on the line. I'll tell you a little bit more beyond that — you need to come to Abraham type faith, where you are willing to put someone else's life on the line; that's what Abraham did. Isn't Abraham the father of faith? What did he put on the line? He put his own son on the line.

I'll never forget when God showed this to me. I know what it feels like, saints. Because I know the time my son

Randy was in a motorcycle accident, I put his life on the line. I didn't realize what I was doing then, but I was putting his life on the line by my believing God. Then, later, my oldest daughter fell on her head, and had a concussion, and all she did was sleep for three days. God spoke to me the very first day and said, "Son, that's Abraham faith." I said, "God, what do You mean?" He said, "You are putting her life on the line." I said, "God, I'm staking her life that there will be no damage to her head and she's going to live; I believe Your Word." The devil said, "She'll die, you dirty, low-down dog; if you had taken her to the doctor she may have lived." Listen, saints, before I would get off of the Word of God I would let her die and go to a better place. Now that is pretty strong, but that's the place you are going to have to come to if you are going to really walk with the Lord in these last days.

In the early days of Christianity the parents had to stand by as their children were thrown to the lions. They would let them throw their children to lions before they would reject Jesus. Years ago there was a preacher in Massachusetts who had a wife and five or six children. They locked him up for preaching the gospel. They were going to stop him from preaching the gospel, and after about four or five weeks his wife and his children were hungry. And you know how they tried to break him? They brought his wife and his children before him, as he was there in prison, and they said, "Now listen, we know that you love your wife and these children. If you will promise that you will quit preaching about Jesus, we will let you out so you can go get a job and support your family." The little children were hungry, and said, "Daddy, we're hungry." He looked through the bars and cried, and said, "Kids, I love you, but I can't go back on Jesus." He wouldn't give up. This is the caliber of Christians God is raising up today.

There is authority and power in the Name of Jesus. It

can keep the tragedies from coming your way. We're talking about protection by angels, and it's supernatural. It will bring you the protection only God can give you — total, complete protection for every situation and circumstance. Oftentimes all you may have time to say is just, "Jesus!" So you must have the Word of God in you. Begin to meditate the Scriptures, and plant them in your heart.

You can probably get a $75 or $100 a month raise in salary by believing in angels. You can save the cost of your premiums. When we came into the knowledge of divine healing, we received a $75 to $100 a month raise. I know one brother who received about a $250 a month raise. He had pills in the medicine cabinet for everyone in the family. They were all taking them day after day. He threw the medicine away and had an extra $250 monthly. Another area is to stop buying on credit, and you can eliminate all interest.

Make this confession: "Lord Jesus Christ, I want You to make me open so that I will be willing to meet any condition so God's angels can protect me and my family and our possessions and our property."

Let me say it again: The devil hates you. You are his eternal enemy, because you believe in Jesus. That makes him desire to kill you. Realize you are not fighting against flesh and blood, so you need something on your side that's not flesh and blood. Your enemy is a spirit; therefore, you don't have any fleshly weapon that can fight against a spirit. Anything you are trying in the natural is ridiculous; it won't work against a spirit. There is only one thing that will work against him, and that is another spirit. He's an unholy spirit, and an angel is a holy angel. Therefore, if you want protection from the evil one, who is out to kill you, you must get your help from God, who is a Spirit, and He will assign His angels to guard and protect you. Can you see what I'm taking about? If you are trying to use natural things to fight against a spirit, how can you do it? You can't see him with your eyes, you can't hit him, you can't feel him; you can't shoot him, you can't knife him; you can't stop him from working any way except through faith in Jesus. Start putting your faith in God's angels, and they will camp on your doorstep, and you will begin to see them with your spiritual eyes, and realize they do minister on your behalf.

I believe in angels, and therefore I have spiritual beings that encamp round about me, to fight the devil for me, and keep him from using automobiles and airplanes and guns and knives and wrecks and the ways of evil men against me. God protects me, and prolongs my days, to give me a full, long life in serving the Lord Jesus Christ.

CHAPTER FOUR
AREAS OF ANGEL PROTECTION
OUTLINE

INTRODUCTION:
Believe angels exist, believe in their ministry of protection, **and** meet the conditions.

I. EVILS FROM WHICH DELIVERANCE IS PROMISED:
1. Psalm 91:3, "Snare of the fowler."
2. Psalm 91:3, "Noisome pestilence."
3. Psalm 91:5, "Terror by night."
4. Psalm 91:5, "Arrow that flieth by day."
5. Psalm 91:6, "Destruction that wasteth at noonday.

II. THE REWARD OF THOSE WHO TRUST GOD:
1. Psalm 91:4, "His truth shall be thy shield and buckler."
2. Psalm 91:5, "Thou shalt not be afraid.

3. Psalm 91:7, "It shall not come nigh thee."
4. Psalm 91:8, "Eyes . . . behold and see the reward of the wicked."
5. Psalm 91:15, "I will answer him . . . in trouble."
6. Psalm 91:15, "I will be with him in trouble."
7. Psalm 91:15, "Honour him."
8. Psalm 91:16, "With long life will I satisfy him."
9. Psalm 91:16, "Shew him my salvation."
10. Luke 10:19, "Give unto you power . . .over all the power of the enemy."
11. I Corinthians 10:13, "God is faithful, who will not suffer you to be tempted above that ye are able; but will with the temptation also make a way to escape . . ."

CHAPTER FOUR
AREAS OF ANGEL
PROTECTION

INTRODUCTION: If God's people do not learn how to exercise faith for angels to protect them, the devil is going to continually be knocking them down, with all kinds of accidents and diseases and everything else. Angels are God's ministering spirits sent to His people. When God sent His Son, Jesus, to pay the price for our sins, He knew that we would live in a world predominantly controlled by Satan. He knew that most of the people in the world were heathen people, people who did not believe in Jesus Christ, and He knew that the devil was going to continually be trying to destroy Christians' lives, because the devil does not want Christians to witness for Jesus. Therefore, God sends His angels to protect His people. Why then aren't more of God's people being protected? **They don't believe in angels!** They think angels are folklore and fairy tale; they picture angels as little babies with wings and rosy cheeks, flapping around somewhere. This is how the devil has deceived God's people. He has made them believe that angels do not exist, or that they do exist but they are not powerful enough. But we are beginning to see in the Bible the power of God's angels. Remember — one of God's angels killed 185,000 men. Now you talk about power — that's power the world doesn't understand. When God's people begin to believe, and get their faith operating in the area of angels, it will work for them. For years Christians didn't believe in divine healing, so it didn't work for them. Some thought the only way you could be healed was by medicine. Then when they learned the Word of God that promised Jesus Christ would heal, they began to exercise faith in divine healing and God started healing. For years many didn't believe God would prosper them; they thought the only way you could prosper was in the world and its system. But they began to learn the Word of God and began to find out that **God** would prosper them. So in every area we are continually reaching forth and learning and receiving more of the revelation of God in Christ Jesus, and angelic ministry is one of the areas.

We talked about the description of angels in chapter one. In chapter two we talked about the ministry of angels, and in chapter three we talked about the conditions for angel protection. Now we are going to consider the areas of angel protection. If angels are going to protect you, in what areas are they going to protect you? If you don't believe they exist, there is no way they can protect you in any area. If you don't believe that God will heal you, well then, God can't heal you; because God always operates on the basis of faith. Many people say, "Well, Brother Willis, I don't believe God would give me enough money to pay my home off." He can't, because you don't believe He will. Most Christians today have what can be called a negative faith. They have faith in cancer to kill, but not God to heal. You can ask them, "Do you believe a cancer will kill?" "Oh, yes, I know a cancer will kill." "Do you believe God will heal it?" Then they are not sure. Now can you imagine a person saying he is a Christian, and having more faith in a cancer to kill than in

64

God to heal? It shows ignorance concerning the Word of God. Therefore, we must believe that angels exist, and believe in their ministry of protection. We dealt with this extensively in the first two chapters. Faith comes by hearing, and hearing by the Word of God. It is only as you take the Word of God and begin to meditate on it that faith will begin to rise in your heart, and you will recognize that angels do exist, and will protect you. Then after you begin to believe they exist, and believe in their ministry, you can meet the conditions. But, first of all, you must believe they exist. Secondly, you must believe that they have a ministry. God created everything for a purpose, and the Bible tells us in Hebrews that angels are ministering spirits sent to minister to God's people.

Psalm 91:4 says, "HIS TRUTH SHALL BE THY SHIELD AND BUCKLER." God's Word is my "buckler," or my armor. His truth is your shield, and His truth is your armor. Through believing the Word of God you put on armor. By the Word of God, faith and trust, you believe God, and His angels move on your behalf. The truth (that angels are real) is the Word of God.

Psalm 91:11 says, "For he shall give his angels charge over thee." I put it in the first person, "over me," to keep **me** in all **my** ways. God said He will give His angels charge over you and me to keep . . . That word "keep" means to guard, to garrison, to protect. Literally this word "keep" means to "garrison something about it"; to take someone and put him inside a stockade and guard him and garrison him, and keep him protected there. God says His angels will literally "garrison you about." They will put you inside of their protective shield, and they will guard you and protect you. You may put someone inside to keep him from getting out; well, God puts His angels around you to keep the devil from getting **in.** Therefore, as you believe in God's Word, He has obligated Himself to perform for you in accordance with His Word. He voluntarily did it, freely exercised His will; no one forced Him to do it. No human being forced God to say He would give His angels charge over thee. All we need to do is believe, and meet the conditions that God sets down.

Psalm 34:7 says, "THE ANGEL OF THE LORD ENCAMPETH ROUND ABOUT THEM THAT FEAR HIM" (those who reverence Him, those who believe His Word, those who trust in Him). God's angels encamp round about them that fear Him. They encamp about, encircle, they surround them that fear Him, and deliver them. What do they deliver you from? The devil, snare of the fowler, the noisome pestilence, the things that come against you.

I. **EVILS FROM WHICH DELIVERANCE IS PROMISED.**

1. In **Psalm 91:3** it says, "SURELY HE SHALL DELIVER THEE FROM THE SNARE OF THE FOWLER." The words, "snare of the fowler," mean "hidden dangers of the cleverest and cruelest of all — Satan"; in other words, Satan's cruelest and cleverest actions. God's angels will deliver you from them.

I Timothy 4:1,2 says in the last days there shall be seducing spirits that shall seduce God's people and lead them astray. The angels will help protect you from the snares of the enemy. One of the snares that would draw you away is wealth. God wants you to prosper, but realize it can draw you away. Many people get prosperous and the next thing that happens is they grow spiritually cold. God wants you to be prosperous, but you don't have to be prosperous and cold; you can be prosperous and fervent in spirit. Position and success may be snares of the fowler, things that he would put there to entice you, and draw you away. A beautiful home; God wants you to have a nice place, but realize it can become a snare. "How do I know if something has snared me?" **Anything you can't get rid of has snared you.** Anything you can't get rid of has

66

power over you. Praise God, His angels will help protect you from the snare of the fowler, the things that would draw you away.

2. **Psalm 91:3,** "SURELY HE SHALL DELIVER THEE . . . FROM THE NOISOME PESTILENCE." This means things that would destroy and cut you off, the things doctors and drugs can't cure, the so-called incurable. God will protect you from these things. When the plagues are on the rampage, the angels will keep these plagues from getting near you. They have power to protect from these noisome pestilences. For example, this covers retardation. God will protect you from the demon spirit of retardation. The angels will do battle for you, and stand for you, and guard you from Satan as he attempts to come against you to snare you and trap you. If you believe God's angels are watching over you, they will keep you from being destroyed, and keep you from being cut off.

3. The angels will deliver you from the "TERROR BY NIGHT." These are the thoughts of the mind; the robber, the rapist, the effects of darkness; especially the thoughts of women concerning rapists breaking in and raping them. When your children are gone off to school and away from home at night time, you better believe in angels. Someone needs to protect them, because the devil is out to get them in trouble, hurt them, or harm them. The Word of God says that surely he shall deliver thee from "THE TERROR BY NIGHT." Darkness has an effect upon nearly everybody, but you can have victory over it. When the devil puts the darts in your mind that somebody is peeping through your window, you won't be disturbed, because you know God's angels are out there. If you really believe your angels are on guard out there, your mind will not become fearful, because you will firmly believe the angels are out there protecting. If you don't believe the angels are out there, your mind is going to start running, and fear takes control. Did you ever

look under the bed? Did you ever check in the closets? God will deliver you from the terror by night, because you say, "Lord, I believe Your angels are protecting me." Do you know why there are more and more alarm systems, etc? Fear! Even Christians have alarm systems, because they do not believe in angels. If you believe in angels, you won't need alarms or detectors of any kind.

4. Here's another thing He will deliver you from . . . the "ARROW THAT FLIETH BY DAY," **Psalm 91:5.** This refers to riots, bullets, attacks, and wars. All over the world there is a lot going on in these areas, and there has been some of it here in the United States. Some say, "Well, I'm going to protect my own." I am, too, but I'm going to protect them God's way — I'm going to believe His angels are going to be there. There are many, many testimonies about how God's angels have protected people. Many people are being killed accidentally, or what they call accidentally. The devil is behind all accidents.

Some Christians may be having difficulty believing in angels. If what God has said in the Word about angels is not true, how do we know the rest of it is true? If angels are myth and folklore, then heaven may be a myth, hell may be a myth. You may not have any place to go when you die; you may just be dead, like an old dog, if there is no heaven or no hell. If you don't believe this part, how do you know the rest of it is true? If anything sounds like a myth, it's streets paved with gold! If anything sounds like fantasy, it's a place where there is no worry and no sickness and no disease, and you just live forever and ever! It's amazing to me how a Christian can believe certain parts of the Bible and get to other parts of it and say no. I believe in angels; I believe in heaven; and the same One Who sent me the book about heaven, sent the book about angels. If He lied about angels, then He may have lied about heaven, too. If He lied about angels He may have lied about hell. That means all those people out there who are living like the devil will never go to hell. Believe in angels just as you do every other area of God's Word.

5. He says in **Psalm 91:6,** Surely He shall deliver thee from "THE DESTRUCTION THAT WASTETH AT NOONDAY." What is the destruction that wasteth at noonday? This is referring to tornadoes, hurricanes, floods, earthquakes, and all kinds of natural destruction. I want you to realize something: God is not behind hurricanes and storms. Jesus **rebuked** the storm, and if God caused the storm then Jesus rebuked something **God** started. He rebuked the wind, he rebuked the sea, and said, "Be still." Jesus said He did only the things God told Him to do. Insurance policies call these things "acts of God." Jesus said in John 10:10 that He came that we might have life and have it more abundantly. When tornadoes and hurricanes come your way, rebuke them. There have been many testimonies about people who rebuked tornadoes when they came their way. They said, "In the name of Jesus, don't you come here," and the thing would jump over their house and come down on the other side of them. God says surely the angels shall deliver thee from the arrow that flieth by day, and from the destruction that wasteth at noonday — floods, earthquakes, etc. God is not behind those things.

II. THE REWARD FOR THOSE WHO TRUST GOD.

1. **Psalm 91:4** says, "HIS TRUTH SHALL BE THY SHIELD AND BUCKLER." In other words, the truth about His angels will help them to be your shield. They will guard off the tornadoes and hurricanes; they will guard off the robbers and the rapists. They will protect you from all these things. Every Believer needs to believe in God's angels.

2. **Psalm 91:5,** "THOU SHALT NOT BE

AFRAID . . .'' It does not say fear does not come against you, but not to be afraid of it. For those who trust in God it says, "THOU SHALT NOT BE AFRAID OF THE TERROR BY NIGHT; NOR OF THE ARROW THAT FLIETH BY DAY." Thou shall **not** be afraid. One of the rewards for believing in God, and believing in His angels, is "Thou shalt not be afraid." II Timothy 1:7 says God has not given you a spirit of fear. Here is what happens. You see circumstances and situations coming your way. You see a car coming your way, or a hurricane, or a tornado. You hear it on TV, you hear it on radio; and what begins to happen? Fear rises! But, praise God, if you have your faith working and you are believing in God's angels, they will protect you from those things. That tree that would fall across your house can fall **beside** your house, or it may fall on the neighbor's house, if he's not in faith.

3. **Psalm 91:7** says, "BUT IT SHALL NOT COME NIGH THEE." It may come close, but not harm those trusting the Lord. He says that no evil shall come nigh thee. It may come close, but it won't harm you.

4. **Psalm 91:8**, "ONLY WITH THINE EYES SHALT THOU BEHOLD AND SEE THE REWARD OF THE WICKED." God is faithful to protect His own; others are left to Satan. This is one of the rewards to the Christian. In days ahead we're going to see what happens to those who know not God. The tornadoes will get them, the hurricanes will get them; the rapists will get them, the robbers will get them, the thieves will get them; the plagues will get them. But if you believe in God's angels and God's Word, then the angels will encamp round about you and God's Word shall protect you, and deliver you from these things. **The devil is rewarding them for serving him, by killing them,** and destroying everything they have.

5. **Psalm 91:15** says, "I WILL ANSWER HIM . . . IN TROUBLE." How do you like that reward? When trouble

comes your way, praise God, the tornadoes, the hurricanes, the robbers and rapists come, you can say, "Glory to God, the angels of the Lord encamp round about me, and no, no, no evil shall befall me." Here's how I confess it all the time: "The angels of the Lord encamp round about me and my family, and our ministry, and possessions and property we're good stewards of, because I abide under the shadow of the Almighty God; and God alone is my refuge, and God alone is my fortress, and God's Word alone is my shield, and God's Word alone is my buckler, my armor." **God is the One in Whom we are trusting** (Proverbs 3:5,6).

6. Notice what else He says. **Psalm 91:15** says, "I WILL BE WITH HIM IN TROUBLE." God says He will be with you. Isaiah 43:1-3 says when you pass through the rivers and waters and fires He will be with you. Hebrews 13:5 says He will never leave you, or never forsake you. So when troubles and problems come your way, remember Jesus is within you. Through faith in God those troubles and problems can't affect you when He is within you. The only way they can plague you is when your faith is not operative, when you don't believe that God is going to protect and take care of you. Before I came to the Lord, I should have been dead a hundred times. It was just the grace of God. But now as Christians, you and I are responsible to learn the Word of God. I praise God, He says He will be with us in trouble. **Philippians 4:19**, "MY GOD SHALL SUPPLY ALL YOUR NEED" (as long as meat doesn't go over $5.00 per pound!). It doesn't make any difference, if you don't believe that you are going to go hungry, because you believe the Word of God.

7. **Psalm 91:15,** "HONOUR HIM." God can honor a man or woman who trusts in Him. He will keep you healthy and strong, spiritually, physically, mentally and financially. He will honor your trust and faith in Him. He

will lift you up, give you miracles, get you out of tough spots and troubles. When others are crying and moaning He will honor you, and you will be rejoicing. When others can't make it, you'll be going right on with the Lord, rejoicing in Him because He said very plainly He will honor him that trusteth in Him.

8. **Psalm 91:16,** "WITH LONG LIFE WILL I SATISFY HIM." Everybody is trying to live a long time, but they do not want to believe that **God** will give them long life. They want to believe the doctors will give them long life. They're going to practice on you to kill you, and charge you while they do it. If they operate on you and you die, they still send a bill. They charge you just as much if you die or live! They will give you a medicine that reacts wrongly and they still send the bill. If it reacts wrongly you get billed for that, and then they give you another one to take care of the reaction, and bill you for that one, too. Suckers! **God** doesn't do you that way. They say, "Go try this (and charge you $20), and if it doesn't work come back, and we'll let you try something else" (and charge you another $20); and they let you come back and charge you $20 every time while they are **trying**. And you are sucker enough to go for it: let them practice on you, and pay them for practicing. They don't promise you long life; they're doing the best they can, but **God** says, "With long life will **I satisfy you**."

In Ephesians 6:1-3, the Bible says for children to honor their parents and their days shall be long. I honor my parents, and my days are going to be long. I respect them, because God has said in His Word, Children, honor your parents and your days shall be long. That is a good prom- ise. I use that for my sons and my daughters; they honor me. When the devil tried to kill my son Randy, I said, "God, Your Word says for children to honor their parents and their days shall be long; and Lord, he honors me."

72

There he lay on the ground, had been in a motorcycle accident and run over, his eyes rolled back in his head; and 18 is not a long life. I had the Word of God, I had something to remind God with; and God healed him and raised him up.

Most people believe that God has appointed unto men once to die — that's right, He did. But He didn't say short of seventy! He says He promises you at least seventy years. And then after that you're on grace; that's better. Grace is better than the promise — that will take you further. Man can't promise you long life; he will do the best he can, but God is the only One Who can promise long life to you.

9. **Psalm 91:16** says, "I WILL SHEW HIM MY SALVATION." In other words, God will reveal to us all that Jesus is. God says, "I will show you My salvation." He says, "I will unfold Jesus to you; I will reveal the Word of God to you."

10. **Luke 10:19**, "BEHOLD, I GIVE UNTO YOU POWER TO TREAD ON SERPENTS AND SCORPIONS, AND OVER ALL THE POWER OF THE ENEMY: AND NOTHING SHALL BY ANY MEANS HURT YOU." He gives us power over all the power of the enemy. Anyway, what is the power of the enemy? John 10:10 says Jesus is come that you might have life and have it more abundantly, and the devil has come to steal, kill and destroy. Jesus says He gives you power over ALL the power of the enemy. That means you have power over all the devil's power to kill, and steal, and destroy you.

11. **I Corinthians 10:13,** "THERE HATH NO TEMPTATION TAKEN YOU BUT SUCH AS IS COMMON TO MAN: BUT GOD IS FAITHFUL, WHO WILL NOT SUFFER YOU TO BE TEMPTED ABOVE THAT YE ARE ABLE; BUT WILL WITH THE TEMPTATION ALSO MAKE A WAY TO ESCAPE, THAT YE MAY BE ABLE

TO BEAR IT." He says he will not permit you to suffer or be tempted more than you are able to bear. The Lord says He will always make a way of escape for you. The angels of the Lord encamp round about them that fear Him (Psalm 34:7).

Let's review. God's angels are created beings, created by God. He created them with a purpose, and they minister to Him and minister throughout the universe in behalf of God's children. God desires us to be healthy, strong, protected, and prosperous. He knows that we're living in the midst of a violent world. He knows that we're living in a world that's predominantly controlled by Satan and the heathenistic system. He knows the devil hates you; he knows the enemy wants to kill you, because the devil doesn't want you to witness to anybody, or doesn't want you to tell anybody that Jesus is Lord. He wants you to keep your mouth shut, and the best way the devil can keep your mouth shut forever is to kill you. He will steal a husband away from a mother with five children so he can mess up the lives of the five children and the wife; steal a wife from a husband and five or six children, and there's a man trying to raise children with no way in the world he can be a mother and a daddy to them. God does not author confusion like that. This is how the devil has messed up so many people today, because they have not believed in the protective power of God's angels. (Psalm 34:7) He very plainly says the angels of the Lord encamp round about them that fear Him. **Psalm 91:11,** "FOR HE SHALL GIVE HIS ANGELS CHARGE OVER THEE, TO KEEP THEE IN **ALL THY WAYS**."

Here is a confession for you: "I believe God's Word, and God's Word says He gives His angels charge over me, to keep me in **all** my ways. The word 'keep' means to garrison, to guard, to encamp around, to keep from the snare of the fowler; to keep from destruction from the devil and the world. This is part of my heirship, part of my inheritance, part of my blessings as a Christian: God has angels that will protect me and my family and our possessions. Father God, I believe Your Word, because if You lied here the whole Bible could be a lie. But I believe You told the truth in all of it, so I believe that wherever I am, or my husband, or my wife, or my children, or my parents, Father God, I am claiming protection for them. I'm claiming that Your angels are right there with them, and any evil that comes against them, I believe Your angels are going to keep it from them, because I claim long life. You said in Psalm 91, with long life, with **long** life, You will satisfy me. Amen.''

One of the ways you can have long life is that you are going to be protected from accidents; from car accidents, from shootings, from plane crashes. I'll never forget an incident that took place a few years ago on a commercial airliner when I was on the way to Oklahoma City for a seminar. A wholesale liquor salesman was sitting next to me. We were about half way to Oklahoma City from Dallas when lightning struck the airplane. He and I were sitting in the front two seats, and we saw that lightning when it struck. It shot through the cabin where the utensils were in the kitchen part, where they serve you drinks and food; we saw smoke puff out from that compartment. Evidently we were the only ones who saw it. We just happened to be looking at it. The stewardess quickly closed the curtain to the kitchen area. The liquor salesman saw the lightning, and fear took control. I said to him, ''Listen, you have nothing to worry about.'' He said, ''What do you mean?'' I said, ''God's angels encamp round about me, and any plane I'm in doesn't go down until it goes down at an airport where we desire to go down.''

You hear about people all the time — somebody runs through a stop sign — some drunk runs a stop sign and kills innocent people. They aren't going to kill me. If they run that stop sign they're going to hit some heathen, some unbeliever. It may even be an unbelieving Christian, because many Christians are getting killed, all the time. Some say, "Well, weren't they Christians?" Sure, but they don't believe in angels. You start talking about angels, and most Christians give you that little stupid look; you know, like anyone who believes in angels has to be ignorant. They are the ones who are ignorant, because the Word of God contains many, many Scriptures concerning angels.

I want you to quote this with me: (Let's just confess it out loud) "**Proverbs 2:8,** 'HE KEEPETH THE PATHS OF JUDGMENT, AND PRESERVETH THE WAY OF HIS SAINTS'"; and that's me, and you (if you are a born-again Christian).

Proverbs 11:8, "THE RIGHTEOUS IS DELIVERED OUT OF TROUBLE, AND THE WICKED COMETH IN HIS STEAD." **You** are the righteousness of God; God says He will deliver the righteous out of trouble. Blue Cross will not protect from tornadoes; it just fixes you up after the tornado tears you up.

Here are a few more Scriptures for you to meditate on.

Proverbs 14:3, "THE LIPS OF THE WISE SHALL PRESERVE THEM." The "lips of the wise" is that person who says, "I believe in angels." That's wise lips — "I **believe** what the Word of God says. I **believe** He will satisfy me with long life; I **believe** the angels of the Lord encamp round about me, and no evil shall befall me."

Proverbs 30:5, "EVERY WORD OF GOD IS PURE: HE IS A SHIELD UNTO THEM THAT PUT THEIR TRUST IN HIM." Suppose they don't put their trust in Him? No shield. It doesn't work; therefore, they have to use something man has to offer.

Psalm 34:7, "THE ANGEL OF THE LORD EN-CAMPETH ROUND ABOUT" me and my family, because

76

I fear Him, and that angel delivereth us. (That's how to put it in the first person.)

Psalm 84:11, "FOR THE LORD GOD IS A SUN AND SHIELD: THE LORD WILL GIVE GRACE AND GLORY: NO GOOD THING WILL HE WITHHOLD FROM THEM THAT WALK UPRIGHTLY." If the angels encamp round about you, that's a good thing.

Psalm 91:10. Confess this with me: "'THERE SHALL NO EVIL BEFALL' me or my family, neither shall any plague come nigh our dwelling." (That's the way to confess that.)

Psalm 91:11-12. Confess this: "'FOR HE SHALL GIVE HIS ANGELS CHARGE OVER' me and my family, to keep all of us, in all our ways. They shall bear us up in their hands, lest we dash our feet against a stone."

Psalm 121:7, "THE LORD SHALL PRESERVE THEE FROM ALL EVIL." Are accidents evil? Are tornadoes evil? What do they do? Kill, steal, and destroy? Anything that kills, steals, and destroys is evil; so the Bible says the Lord will preserve you from all evil. Then you start believing the Word of God for Him to make you healthier than what you are now.

Luke 10:19, "BEHOLD, I GIVE UNTO YOU (God gives unto me) POWER TO TREAD ON SERPENTS AND SCORPIONS (that means the devil and demons), AND OVER ALL THE POWER OF THE ENEMY; AND **NOTHING** SHALL BY ANY MEANS HURT YOU (me or my family)." He says He gives you power and authority over all the power of the enemy, and nothing shall by any means hurt you.

Father, we thank You that faith is rising to believe in Your Word about the protecting power of angels. Father, I claim the protection of Your angels for each individual who reads this study guide, and receives the message of total protection. Amen.

CHAPTER FIVE
INCREASING LIFE'S SPAN

OUTLINE

I. KNOW GOD'S PLAN:
1. Psalm 90:10, "The days of our years are three-score years and ten: and if by reason of strength they be fourscore years . . ."
2. Exodus 23:26, "The number of thy days I will fulfill."

II. KNOW GOD'S CONDITIONS:
1. Proverbs 4:10, "Hear . . . and receive my sayings (not the world's); and the years of thy life shall be many."
2. Proverbs 3:1-2, "Forget not my law; but let thine heart keep my commandments: for length of days, and long life, and peace, shall they add to thee."
3. III John 2, "Beloved, I wish (pray) above all things that thou mayest prosper and be in health even as thy soul prospereth."

III. KNOW GOD IS THE REAL SOURCE OF HEALTH AND LIFE:
Medicines are man's efforts to stay alive without trusting God.
1. Exodus 15:26, "I am the Lord that healeth

thee."

2. Proverbs 9:11, "For by me thy days shall be multiplied, and the years of thy life shall be increased."

3. Psalm 121:7, "The Lord shall preserve thee from all evil."

4. Proverbs 10:27, "The fear of the Lord prolongeth days; but the years of the wicked shall be shortened."

5. II Timothy 4:18, "The Lord shall deliver me from every evil work, and will preserve me unto his heavenly kingdom."

6. Proverbs 2:8, "He preserveth the way of his saints."

7. Psalm 103:4, "Who redeemeth thy life from destruction."

8. Psalm 91:16, "With long life will I satisfy him."

IV. **KNOW WHERE STRENGTH COMES FROM:**

1. Psalm 90:10, "If by reason of strength they be fourscore . . ."

2. Psalm 28:7-8, "The Lord is my strength and shield . . . and he is the saving strength of his anointed."

3. Isaiah 26:4, "In the Lord God is everlasting strength."

4. II Timothy 4:17, "The Lord stood with me and strengthened me."

V. **KNOW FAITH MUST BE OPERATIVE TO REAP THE BENEFITS:**

1. **God's promises:**

   II Corinthians 1:20, "All the promises of God in him are yea, and in him Amen, unto the glory of God by us."

   * Psalm 91:11, "For he shall give his angels charge over thee, to keep thee in all thy

ways."

*Psalm 34:7, "The angel of the Lord encampeth round about them that fear him, and delivereth them."

2. God's principle:

Romans 10:17, "So then faith cometh by hearing, and hearing by the Word of God."

*Numbers 23:19, "God is not a man, that he should lie."

*Isaiah 55:11, "My word . . . shall not return unto me void."

CHAPTER FIVE
INCREASING LIFE'S SPAN

INTRODUCTION: God desires His children to live a full life. He wants you to be blessed in everything that you say and do. And it's just not necessarily years that help you to be blessed by God, but there's no doubt that the longer we live for the Lord, and study the Word of God, the more intimately we become acquainted with God. As you become acquainted more with God's Word, you become acquainted with God. The more time you have to put in His Word, and study His Word, and meditate His Word, the Word of God becomes more a part of you. God's Word is a direct description of God Himself — it **is** God Himself, expressing His attributes and nature to mankind. I'm learning that the longer I serve the Lord, the longer I study the Word of God, the longer I meditate the Word of God, more mellowing takes place in my life. Things that should not be in my life are laid aside, and the things that need to be there God begins to put in, because we human beings, with our natural minds and natural ways of thinking, rebel against the Spirit and against the spiritual truths of God.

For so long mankind has been taught that maybe he will live a long life, and maybe he won't. God has promised a long life to the people who will walk in His ways. Realize you must meet the conditions, but God has promised long life to those who will obey His Word. He has promised the Christian heaven, and I believe that. Well, saints, "ALL THE PROMISES OF GOD IN HIM ARE YEA, AND IN HIM AMEN, UNTO THE GLORY OF GOD BY US" (II Corinthians 1:20). You will discover in this chapter many Scriptures that will help you lay a foundation for a long life. It doesn't make any difference if you are young or old at this present time. If you're young, you need to get hold of the Scriptures more, because you have more years to live. And if you're on up in years, well praise God, you want to keep yours stretching right on out, and receive **all** of the years the Lord has promised you in His Word.

I. **KNOW GOD'S PLAN:** Realize, if you are going to increase life's span, you must know God's plan.

1. **Psalm 90:10** says, "THE DAYS OF OUR YEARS ARE THREESCORE YEARS AND TEN." Just a few special ones make it threescore and ten: that's what most people believe. The Bible says, "THE DAYS OF **OUR** YEARS . . ." I confess, "The days of **my** life are threescore and ten," and threescore is 60, and 10 make 70, 70 years of age. "AND IF BY REASON OF STRENGTH THEY BE FOURSCORE YEARS" (80). Many take the Scripture referring to Moses and say, "One hundred and twenty years." That's all right with me, too. If you want to go ahead and receive 120, fine; you can have it. Jesus said, "IF THOU CANST BELIEVE, ALL THINGS ARE POSSIBLE TO HIM THAT BELIEVETH" (Mark 9:23). Begin to realize that God wants you to live at **least** 70 years.

2. **Exodus 23:26** says, "THE NUMBER OF THY DAYS I WILL FULFIL." Psalm 90:10 says the number of our years are threescore and ten. Then the Word says in Exodus 23:26, the number of **our** days (**my** days and **your** days) God says He will fulfil; He says He will com-

plete them. Now many people say, "Well, I don't want to live in this world all that long; life is too rough." Saints, I want you to know through Jesus Christ, the Son of God, as you begin to walk with Him and His Word begins to burst forth out of you, and you begin to realize who you are and what you are, **life is good.** Because Jesus is good! Begin to realize that Jesus Christ lives inside of you, and will give you a good, fulfilling life down here. Natural life can be fulfilling, but only as you serve the Lord Jesus Christ. There is no other way to find total fulfillment in life.

When you were made, there was a missing piece of the puzzle in your life. Your whole life is a puzzle, and there is one piece (right in the center) missing, and the only thing that can fill that space is God. He says that He will fulfill the years of our life. You need to recognize that God's plan is anywhere from 70 upward, a minimum 70 years for God's people, **if they will believe Him.**

II. **KNOW GOD'S CONDITIONS.** Secondly, you must know God's conditions to increase your life's span. The conditions are set forth in the Word of God.

1. **Proverbs 4:10,** "HEAR, O MY SON, AND RECEIVE MY SAYINGS; AND THE YEARS OF THY LIFE SHALL BE MANY." You need to hear His sayings as you confess the Scriptures with your mouth. **You need to hear yourself say what the Word of God says.** Proverbs 4:10 says, Hear and receive God's sayings, not the world's sayings. What the world tells you will **never** agree with the Word of God. Notice the condition. Hear — this is why we have published this study guide, that you **might hear the Word** concerning God's angels and their ministry.

2. **Proverbs 3:1-2** says, "FORGET NOT MY LAW." Forget **not** my law; forget not my Word, "BUT LET THINE HEART KEEP MY COMMANDMENTS: FOR LENGTH OF DAYS, AND LONG LIFE, AND PEACE,

SHALL THEY ADD TO THEE." Not only length of days, long life, but also peace. What is the condition? Forget not God's law. So many people forget God's Word. For a season they remember it, and then for a season they forget it. When you forget God's law or God's Word and its desire to bless you, you are putting yourself out from under the Word of God, and the door for the devil to work on you, spiritually, physically, mentally and financially, is opened. Meditate upon God's Word both day and night (Joshua 1:8).

3. **III John 2**, "BELOVED, I WISH (pray) ABOVE ALL THINGS THAT THOU MAYEST PROSPER AND BE IN HEALTH, EVEN AS THY SOUL PROSPERETH." The Lord says He wants you to be in health and prosper. How? even as thy soul prospers. God's Word is true, but it has built-in protections for it to work for you. This one Scripture applies to prosperity and health. God has built-in protections for His Word, built-in conditions. It is only as His children meet the conditions that God will begin to move for them. If you don't believe in angels, then you haven't met the conditions. God will not move for you. If you're not hearing and receiving His Word concerning long life, or angels protecting you, then they won't work for you. It's only as you begin to hear and receive the Word of God that it begins to work for you. Therefore, you must meet the conditions. There are always conditions. One of the conditions for prosperity is giving (Luke 6:38); another is seeking first the kingdom (Matthew 6:33). What is the condition to be saved? "WHOSOEVER SHALL CALL UPON THE NAME OF THE LORD SHALL BE SAVED" (Romans 10:13). Is there a condition for the baptism of the Holy Ghost? Yes; "ASK, AND YOU SHALL RECEIVE" (Luke 11:9-13). Is there a condition for divine healing? Yes, believe Jesus Christ died for your sins and sicknesses (I Peter 2:24). It is only as Believers learn the conditions

and meet the conditions, that the promises become fulfilled in their lives. There are no exceptions to what God promises you. Whatever you find God promises you in His Word, there are no exceptions to it. But there are conditions that must be fulfilled in order for the promise to become yours, for it to manifest itself in your life. In order for you to have healing, there are conditions you must meet. You must believe on the Lord Jesus Christ, believe that by the stripes of Jesus you were healed at Calvary (Isaiah 53:4,5). If you don't believe that by the stripes of Jesus you were healed at Calvary, then you haven't met God's condition; therefore, you cannot receive the promise. The conditions are: hear, receive, forget not, keep my commandments, and you will prosper and be in health even as thy soul prospers (your mind, your will, and your emotions make up your soulish nature). How do they prosper? As your mind is renewed by the Word of God, then your mind, will, and emotions are brought under control of the Word of God. Then you are not disobeying the Word of God, you're living in peace and harmony with the Word, and as you do this your soul prospers and the Word becomes a reality to you.

III. **KNOW GOD IS THE REAL SOURCE OF HEALTH AND LIFE:** The third thing you must know if you're going to have your life span increased, and move in the fulness that God has for you, you must know that God is the real source of health and life. Medicines are man's efforts to stay alive without trusting God. They are man's efforts. **God doesn't need a drug to heal you. Man** needs a drug to heal you, because man can't do it by faith in God. Man doesn't have power to do it through God, so he has to create or make something that will work on your system to cause it to function right; and they've done a good job, in the natural. At the same time, people are dying every day. Man needs to realize that God is the real source of health.

1. **Exodus 15:26**, "I AM THE LORD THAT HEALETH THEE." God is speaking to His people. God says, "I am the Lord that healeth thee." **God** is the One Who heals. If you don't know God, then you can get your healing from man. You see, man says, "Man healeth me; the pills healeth me; drugs healeth me; operations healeth me." But a Christian can say, "**GOD is my healer.**" For He says, "I am the Lord your God that heals you. I am the One that makes you whole." God can do a good job of it. There must be the realization that God is the real source of health and the real source of life. God is the One Who has given you life, and God is the only One Who can keep that life going. Man didn't give you life; man didn't put that life-giving power inside of you. Man is not the giver — God is the Giver of Life. God is the One Who can keep life in you moving forward, as you recognize He is the source. Most people today can't really live a long life, because they do not believe that God is the real source of it. They are trusting in man, and when you trust in man you are going to be disappointed, I guarantee you. It's not because they want to disappoint you. There's not a doctor in any hospital who doesn't want to heal all the sick people. They'd like to have miracle drugs (as they call them) that would heal every disease. But the only One Who can guarantee you healing is the Almighty, Eternal God. He says, "I am the Lord that healeth thee"; He doesn't say, I am the Lord that maketh thee sick! "God killed so-and-so in my family!" No; He says, "I am the Lord that healeth thee"; healing makes you alive, not dead. Healing is health; healing is life unto you. Recognize the fact that Satan is the one who KILLS, STEALS, AND DESTROYS (John 10:10).

2. **Proverbs 9:11** says, "FOR BY ME THY DAYS SHALL BE MULTIPLIED, AND THE YEARS OF THY LIFE SHALL BE INCREASED." Do you know what man says? By drugs, and pills, and proper foods, and proper

exercises, thy days shall be increased. All these things are important. The Word of God says, "BODILY EXERCISE PROFITETH LITTLE," but that little is important. God is the source of my strength; I am healthy and strong not because I exercise, not because I lift weights, not because I jog, not because I eat the right foods; now all these are a part of it, but I'm healthy and strong because God is the source of my strength and the source of my life. I don't give exercise or anything else credit for it. "BY **ME** (God says) THY DAYS SHALL BE MULTIPLIED, AND THE YEARS OF THY LIFE SHALL BE INCREASED." I'm trusting **God** to multiply my days, and the years of my life **shall** be increased. God's Word is true.

3. **Psalm 121:7** says, "THE LORD SHALL PRE-SERVE THEE FROM ALL EVIL." Diseases, accidents, calamities — all these things do not preserve, they destroy. This Scripture plainly says the Lord shall preserve (take care of) you.

4. **Proverbs 10:27,** "THE FEAR OF THE LORD PROLONGETH DAYS." A reverence of the Lord and belief in His Word aid in prolonging your life on this earth. The verse continues, "BUT THE YEARS OF THE WICKED SHALL BE SHORTENED." What is continually happening to man's life span? It is getting shorter and shorter. The tragedy is that God's people have believed what the ungodly believe, and because they believe as the heathen, and the wicked, they too have their days shortened. Your natural mind has been so trained and programmed, all your life, by the world, to think you might die any time. The Word of God promises threescore and ten years, and anything less is not God's will.

5. **II Timothy 4:18** says, "AND THE LORD SHALL DELIVER ME FROM EVERY EVIL WORK." Is sickness evil? It will kill you, won't it? John 10:10 says Jesus has come that you might have life and have it more abun-

dantly, and that the devil has come to steal, kill and destroy. So we can see from this Scripture that the Lord shall deliver us from everything that steals, kills or destroys. Do you know why, in the past, we have not been delivered from every evil work? We did not believe; we were not exercising faith or believing God to deliver us from them. We thought we were lucky. In reality, it was just the grace of God, keeping us alive. But today you can say, "God, I know Your Word, and You said You shall deliver me from every evil work and preserve me." So that means when evil works begin to come your way, don't accept them. It may appear like evil is going to come out of a situation. Say, "No, I refuse that in the name of Jesus; God's Word says He delivers me from **every** evil work." When anything that is evil begins to come against me, I say, "God, You said You would deliver me from **every** evil work." If He said He was going to deliver me from every evil work, then what is He putting sickness on me for? Is He going to deliver me from His Own evil work? Many people believe today that God puts sickness on people. If He does, He must deliver them from His Own evil work. On the other hand, if the **devil** puts that sickness on you, then God is the One Who delivers you from every evil work. Stand upon the Word of God, that He is the real source of health and life. The only way that you can really begin to exercise faith for angels, and for protection, is you will have to get the Word in your heart.

6. **Proverbs 2:8**, "HE PRESERVETH THE WAY OF HIS SAINTS." The ones who are born of God are the children of God, and what does He do for them? Preserveth their way. I thank God He preserves my way; how about you? You shouldn't start a day off without confessing God's protection, because the devil is out there to knock your block off, no matter your age or status in life. You should be confessing every day that God's angels encamp

round about you and your family, and that NO evil shall befall you or your family. Someone in your family needs to start exercising faith. You may say, "Brother Willis, my daddy doesn't believe in it." Well, you do; therefore, take care of dad by the confession of your mouth concerning protection. If **you** believe, then you can exercise faith for your family.

7. **Psalm 103:4** says, "WHO REDEEMETH THY LIFE FROM DESTRUCTION." Redeem means to deliver. God is the One Who delivers your life from all destruction.

8. **Psalm 91:16**, "WITH LONG LIFE WILL I SATISFY HIM." To prevent the things the enemy would bring to kill you, and destroy you before the appointed time, learn the Word of God and you can stand upon it, because God promises long life. It gives me peace to know that God is going to satisfy my sons, and my daughters, and my grandsons and my granddaughters with long life. It's peaceful to know that God is going to satisfy you with long life; it's peaceful to know that you are not living in the fear of death. It's peaceful when you are not worried that maybe tomorrow some accident might kill you. It produces a peace in your heart to know when you take a trip with your family that the angel of the Lord is there to protect your family. Realize the only thing that's going to keep you healthy and strong is the knowledge of the Word of God planted in your heart. You must begin to meditate that Word.

Confess this: "I believe God's Word, and I believe He delivers me and my family from destruction, and He preserveth our way, and He's going to satisfy us with long life — long, long life. Amen."

IV. **KNOW WHERE STRENGTH COMES FROM:**

1. **Psalm 90:10**, "THE DAYS OF OUR YEARS ARE THREESCORE YEARS AND TEN; AND IF BY REASON OF STRENGTH THEY BE FOURSCORE." Where does

this strength come from? For you to get on up in years is going to require strength. Because the body begins to wear out; and really there is no reason it should wear out except for sin and Satan. When God made the body, it was made to live eternally. Even after Adam sinned he lived for years and years. Many men lived 800 and 900 years. Well, what was the difference then? Sin through the years began to take its toll. Their bodies (Adam and Eve) just kept on reproducing themselves, somewhat like a tree. But sin has stopped that process. God says, "IF BY REASON OF STRENGTH THEY BE FOURSCORE YEARS." From 80 on up you're on grace. You have a promise to 70; above 70 you are on grace; and grace is better. Therefore, really you ought to be able to do better than 80.

2. **Psalm 28:7-8** says, "THE LORD IS MY STRENGTH AND MY SHIELD . . ." Verse 8 says, the Lord "IS THE SAVING STRENGTH OF HIS ANOINTED." He is the strength of His children, His anointed ones. I confess this all the time: "The **Lord** is my strength; I am strong and healthy. I eat right, I exercise, I do all those natural things; but that's not why I'm strong. That just keeps the rust out. I'm strong because the **Lord is my strength**. He gives His beloved restful sleep, and that's me." The Scripture doesn't say He gives you just sleep; it says restful sleep. There's a lot of difference between sleep and restful sleep. I get restful sleep. When you get restful sleep, it doesn't take very much of it. One reason so many people need so much sleep is that they do not sleep restfully. They turn and toss and roll and tumble, and have all kinds of nightmares and dreams and everything else. That is not restful sleep. Restful sleep is when you go to bed and you sleep. Suppose you wake up tomorrow and it wasn't restful sleep? Well, how does the devil know? I don't tell him. I just say, "Father God, I praise Your name for that good solid, sound, restful sleep." I want to tell you

something the Lord showed me about sleep. Just before you wake up in the morning, here is what the devil will do. Thirty minutes or an hour before you wake up, he goes to work on your mind, and you roll and tumble for twenty or thirty minutes and he makes you think you've been rolling and tumbling all night long. That is exactly his tactics. God showed that to me in 1973. He showed it to me and I began to realize the enemy's tactics, so every morning I would wake up and say, "God, I thank You for that good sound, restful sleep." But the devil put it in my mind that I had rolled and tumbled all night long. I thought I had it in my mind, but God had shown me differently. God had shown me that he attacked just for a season, and caused me to roll and tumble and planted it in my mind. So I make my confession: "Thank You, Lord, for my good, solid, sound, restful sleep." I began to observe that as I really took hold of that principle, I didn't have any more tired days because I had rolled and tossed all night. If I believed a lie, that I rolled and tumbled all night long, what did I receive? I dragged all day. But, if I believed the truth, that God had given me good sound, restful sleep, I was alert all day. Sometimes at first it would take my body a while to get going because the devil had planted it so strongly in my mind. Most people can't go beyond the knowledge in their minds. If their mind says they didn't sleep, well, their body says the same thing, and they struggle all day because the mind will make the body tired. You start talking to some-body about being sick, and soon you can talk their mind into being sick, and next thing you know their body feels sick. You can get a group of people that are tired around somebody who is not tired, and they can all start talking about being tired and dragging, and next thing you know the one who is not tired will be tired and dragging. So what the devil does is plant thoughts in your mind. If you believe what's in your mind above the promise of God, then you void God's promise to work for you. And the truth is, praise God, God's Word works for you but the devil simply steals the truth of the Word of God from you. So you need to recognize these things. Remember, the **Lord** is your strength and your shield.

3. **Isaiah 26:4,** "IN THE LORD GOD IS EVER-LASTING STRENGTH." That's going to last as long as you and I are here on the earth — everlasting strength. In whom do we have this strength? In the Lord God is ever-lasting strength; not in man, not in exercise, not in the pill, but in the Lord God. In God is eternal life, and also in Him is everlasting strength. In Him is health; in Him is power; in Him is authority; in Him is anointing. Everything that you need, it is in HIM, in Jesus Christ, the Son of God. The LORD is the strength of your life. Everyone needs to confess this every day, "God, You are my everlasting strength." God lives in me, He energizes my body. You can go to the doctor and he can give you a shot and put vitamins in your body, but the Holy Spirit will put strength in your body. He energizes your body with strength; He energizes your body with life; He energizes your body with health. But it won't work for you if you don't believe it. We have been taught all our lives to believe something else — Satan's lies.

4. **II Timothy 4:17** says, "THE LORD STOOD WITH ME, AND STRENGTHENED ME." That's what the Apostle Paul teaches, "The Lord stood with me and strengthened my body." You say, "Well, Brother Willis, it's just not working for me." Well, have you been confessing the Scriptures? The Word is where the life is, so you need to say, "The **Lord** stood with me and strengthened me."

I want you to confess this: "The **Lord** is my strength; He keeps me healthy; He delivers me, and He protects me from evil. He preserves me, healthy, and strong. It's God's will for me to have length of days, and long life, and I claim it. Amen."

V. **KNOW FAITH MUST BE OPERATIVE TO REAP THE BENEFITS:** O.K., here's the fifth thing you must know now if you want to increase your life span. You must know that faith must be operative to reap the benefits. We've been talking about this, but I just want to spend a little time here to close out on it. You must know faith must be operative to reap the benefits. In other words, your faith must know God's promises.

1. **God's promises: II Corinthians 1:20** says, "FOR ALL THE PROMISES OF GOD IN HIM ARE YEA, AND IN HIM AMEN, UNTO THE GLORY OF GOD BY US." All of God's promises (including the promise of long life) are in Him yea and Amen to the glory of God by us. But how is it to God's glory by us? When we believe and receive it, our lives are testimonies of it. Amen? Strong, healthy bodies are a testimony to the glory of God, for God's people. Now you may be reading this study guide and be 70 years of age. Well, praise God, you are on grace now. You are promised 70, but now you are living on grace, and grace is good. "FOR BY GRACE ARE YE SAVED THROUGH FAITH; AND THAT NOT OF YOURSELVES: IT IS THE GIFT OF GOD; NOT OF WORKS, LEST ANY MAN SHOULD BOAST (Ephesians 2:8,9). It's by grace you are saved, and by grace you are kept to live to be 70. The enemy tries to steal the desire for life, as people grow older. As the years go by he will try to get you to settle down, more and more and more. I've become more and more convinced that the further we go with God, the better life becomes.

Psalm 91:11, "FOR HE SHALL GIVE HIS ANGELS CHARGE OVER THEE, TO KEEP THEE IN ALL THY WAYS." God gives His ANGELS charge over us. I praise God that **He** does that. The angels of God keep me in all my ways, as I live on this earth.

Psalm 34:7 says, "THE ANGEL OF THE LORD EN-CAMPETH ROUND ABOUT THEM THAT FEAR HIM (or them that trust in Him), AND DELIVERETH THEM." All those who fear the Lord, respect, and have reverence for God, and who He is: it says God assigns an angel to camp around them.

2. **God's principle.** It's a faith principle. Romans 10:17, "SO THEN FAITH COMETH BY HEARING, AND HEARING BY THE WORD OF GOD." Faith comes by what? Hearing, and hearing by the what? Word of God. Take that Word of God (the Bible) and hear it; take the Word of God and confess it. Say things like this: "The Lord is my strength; He preserveth the way of His saints; With long life will He satisfy me." You say it and you hear it, and you hear it, and you hear it. I confess the Word of God every day for myself and my family. I'm confessing it because, praise God, I want them to live a long time.

Numbers 23:19, "GOD IS NOT A MAN, THAT HE SHOULD LIE; NEITHER THE SON OF MAN, THAT HE SHOULD REPENT: HATH HE SAID, AND SHALL HE NOT DO IT? OR HATH HE SPOKEN, AND SHALL HE NOT MAKE IT GOOD?" The Word of God says He will give us long life. God also says, "I am not a man that I should lie, neither the son of man that I should repent." He says, "I won't change my mind about my Word." Do you know what God says in **Malachi 3:6?** He says, "I AM THE LORD, **I CHANGE NOT**." He hasn't changed from giving His angels charge over you and me since He spoke the Word. He hasn't changed from having His angels encamp round about us. He hasn't changed that He is our strength, He is our life, He is our protection. God has not changed; man has changed. Praise God, many people are beginning to believe God, and take Him at His Word.

Isaiah 55:11, God says, "MY WORD . . . SHALL

NOT RETURN UNTO ME VOID." What is His Word? The Bible we have today is the Word of God. God says in **Malachi 3:6,** "I AM THE LORD, I CHANGE NOT." **Hebrews 13:8,** I am "THE SAME YESTERDAY, AND TODAY AND FOR EVER." You can be sure the Father, Son, and the Spirit all bear witness. In **John 16:13**, Jesus said when the Holy Spirit, "THE SPIRIT OF TRUTH, IS COME, HE WILL GUIDE YOU INTO ALL TRUTH." Guide you into what kind of truth? The truth that God's angels encamp round about you. The truth that by the stripes of Jesus you were healed at Calvary. The truth that God loves you. The truth that He that is in you is greater than he that is in the world. The truth that you are more than a conqueror through Christ Jesus. The truth is that God's angels do encamp round about you. The truth is that He will guide you into all truth. The truth is that whatever you give, He will multiply it back to you, good measure, pressed down, shaken together and running over. You see, saints, we have been foolish to believe the part about heaven and not believe the part that He promises us good things now in this life. Let's cash in on all the benefits. The world says (and some Christians), "Well, you're being selfish." No, as I live in health, I'm a testimony that God keeps His Word. It is wisdom — to believe the Word of God. If your husband doesn't believe it, or your wife doesn't believe it, or your sons and daughters — **you** exercise **your** faith, and keep them protected and keep them with long life until they do come to God. Then when they come to God they will start hearing the Word and come into agreement with you.

Saints, it's for your benefit to desire long life. It's an amazing thing how hard it is sometimes to try to talk people into believing for long life, trying to convince them into believing the Word of God to increase their life span. It's amazing the problems people have when you are trying to get them to believe the angels will protect them. You know

97

if I had been trying to sell them some insurance to die by, it would be different; but you try to teach them the Word of God, that angels are real, and they kind of look at you out of the corners of their eyes. I've had so many people look at me out of the corners of their eyes for a number of years now, because I say I believe in angels. God said it; that settles it, whether anyone ever believes it. Whether you and I believe it or not, it is still true. However, it is only as you and I believe it that we get the benefits. It is only as you believe that by the stripes of Jesus you were healed at Calvary that you can receive the benefits. I don't care what your age is, God wants you to have a good life. God loves you, you are precious to Him; can you picture a father who loves his children so much he would give up one of his sons for them, and yet not want them to have a good life? Especially when it is in his power to give it to them. Now if it's not in the man's power to give it to them, that's one thing; but, brothers and sisters, it's within God's power to give His children abundant, victorious, overcoming life through Christ Jesus. If your relationship is not as it should be with your husband, with your wife, with your son, your daughter, with mom or dad, I want you to know that Jesus will restore that relationship. He will mend the fences, He will patch up the gaps, He will put bridges across the rivers that need to be crossed, so you can walk in the fulness of the things of God and know that He is alive.

Start believing in protection, and hold fast to it; because somewhere along the line the devil is going to try to destroy you. Victory will come, as you stand upon the Word of God. God said it — I believe it — and THAT settles it! Keep shouting the victory.

God is **never** wrong. People are trying to make the Word line up with their experiences. I don't care **what** your experiences are, if your experience doesn't line up with the Word of God, you missed it. The quicker you learn that, the quicker you will repent and begin to walk in victory. Pride will keep you from admitting it — pride will say, "Don't admit you were wrong." Then do you realize what you are saying? God was wrong. If you don't admit you're wrong, that **you** missed it, and God's Word i still true, you are blaming it on God, saying. "God, You didn't uphold Your end of the bargain." Be assured, saints, He upholds His end of the bargain every time.

I want you to make a confession: "Thank You, God, my angels are around me. Hello, Angels of God! Thank you that you are with me always, everywhere I go — in the car, at home, on the job, in the air, on the ground; you are with me. Praise God. God has charged His angels to protect me and my family, and our possessions and property that we are good stewards of. Amen."

CHAPTER SIX
MAINTAINING PROTECTION
OUTLINE

INTRODUCTION

I. CONSISTENT MEDITATION FOR MIND RENEWAL:

Psalm 1:1, "His delight is in the law of the Lord, and in his law doth he meditate day and night."

* Joshua 1:8, "That thou mayest observe to do according to all that is written therein."

II. CONSISTENT CONFESSION FOR FAITH OPERATION:

Proverbs 2:10, "When wisdom entereth into thine **heart**."

* In the heart wisdom is light, life and power.
* In the mind only, wisdom is dry, barren, and speculative, with no practical life changing influence.
* It is "the man whose delight is in the word of the Lord," who is preserved from "walking in the counsel of the ungodly."
* In the heart, Scripture is not just an external rule, but a preserving, keeping principle. Once it was an object of search, but now found it has practical

life changing influence, power, and **pleasure**.

III. STOP THINKING FEAR POSSIBILITIES OR SUPPOSITIONS:

If Satan gets his seed planted, and it is not aborted, it will give birth.

* Psalm 121:7, "The Lord shall preserve thee from all evil."
* II Timothy 4:18, "The Lord shall deliver me from every evil work.'
* Psalm 34:7; Psalm 91:11
* James 4:7, "Submit yourselves therefore to God. Resist the devil, and he will flee from you."

IV. STOP TALKING FEAR:

Words reflect the thoughts of the mind, and reveal to Satan his effectiveness.

* Fear is Satan's weapon to birth doubt.

V. ACT IN WAYS THAT DEMONSTRATE TRUST AND CONFIDENCE IN GOD:

Impossible to do III, IV, V **if** I and II are not in operation.

* Hebrews 11:6, Rewards diligence.
* Philippians 1:6, "Being confident of this very thing, that he which hath begun a **good work in you** will perform it until the day of Jesus Christ."
* Hebrews 10:35-36, "Cast not away therefore your confidence, which hath great recompence of reward. For ye have need of patience, that, **after** ye have done the will of God, ye might receive the promise."
* Isaiah 51:7, "No weapon that is formed against thee shall prosper."

CHAPTER SIX
MAINTAINING PROTECTION

INTRODUCTION: It is one thing to get protection, but something else to keep it. The purpose of this study guide concerning angels is to begin to lay the Word of God before you, so you can build a foundation to stand upon. Your faith cannot operate beyond your knowledge of the Word of God. This book contains many Scriptures on protection by angels. As you ground your faith on the Word of God, be it for spiritual, physical, mental or financial things, angels or anything else, God's Word will begin to work for you. I am sharing with you the Word of God, because I want you to maintain protection. I want you to have a long life. I want you to have a good life. The foundation of that good life is Jesus. Now, it's good to love God, but that's not enough; you must have a knowledge of His Word. Learn God's Word in all the various areas, because His Word always produces. Many years ago as I began to learn the Word of God, I would open the Bible upside down, and I'd start to preach a message. I was so ignorant I would have to flip through the index to find the book of the Bible I was looking for. But I began to learn God's Word and I began to study God's Word, and His Word began to get into my mind. Next thing I knew it began to be planted in my heart. And next thing I knew I began to speak to the mountains, and the mountains began to dissolve and move, in the name of Jesus. I began to **speak** to fear, and frustration, confusion, defeat, hurt, disappointment and discouragement. I began to **speak** to poverty; I began to **speak** to sickness, and all those mountains moved right out into the middle of the sea and drowned, because of the power in the name of Jesus. That same principle is available to all of God's children. It's not just for **me** to have protection by angels, or me to be able to speak the Word. It is the inherited right of every born-again believer to walk in the fulness of the things of God. There are no special elect; it's available for the man or woman who learns God's Word.

In **Psalm 91:1** it says, "HE THAT DWELLETH IN THE SECRET PLACE OF THE MOST HIGH SHALL ABIDE UNDER THE SHADOW OF THE ALMIGHTY." The word "dwelleth" means he that stays, he that remains. Psalm 91:9,10 — "BECAUSE THOU **HAST** MADE THE LORD, WHICH IS MY REFUGE, EVEN THE MOST HIGH, THY HABITATION; THERE SHALL NO EVIL BEFALL THEE, NEITHER SHALL ANY PLAGUE COME NIGH THY DWELLING." No evil shall befall you because "thou **hast** made" the Lord God thy refuge. There must be constant dwelling and abiding in the presence of God. Once you hear the teaching on protection and you begin to move forward, many times the devil knocks your block off. Why? Because you are not dwelling in the secret place, you are not staying in the Word of God concerning protection. If you are going to maintain protection, you must meditate and confess the Scriptures concerning protection. (See Scriptures listed in Foreword.) Stay with the Scriptures until they become alive and personal to **you**, until they begin to shine inside of you and become a reality to **you**. Then you will have made **Him** your refuge, and then you will have made **Him** your fortress; then you will be dwelling, staying, remaining under the shadow of the Almighty God, and the Word of God will work for you. A close fellowship and relationship with the Lord is necessary in order for His Word to work. A close relationship and fellowship with the Lord will help you when Satan attempts to draw you from "under His wings" by bringing fear, worry, or confusion. Your close relationship to the Lord stands as a guard against the enemy.

I. **CONSISTENT MEDITATION FOR MIND RE-NEWAL:** If you are going to maintain the protection of God's angels, the first thing necessary is consistent meditation of the Word of God to renew your mind. I know many may say they have heard all about renewal of the mind. Hearing it and knowing it are two different things. In any area there are principles, and the principle for protection by angels is that your mind must be renewed by the Word of God.

Psalm 1:1,2 — "BLESSED IS THE MAN THAT WALKETH NOT IN THE COUNSEL OF THE UN-GODLY, NOR STANDETH IN THE WAY OF SINNERS, NOR SITTETH IN THE SEAT OF THE SCORNFUL. BUT HIS DELIGHT IS IN THE LAW OF THE LORD; AND IN HIS LAW DOTH HE MEDITATE DAY AND NIGHT." It is only the individual whose delight is in the Word of God, who has that Word continually working for him. Every Christian must come to the place where he knows the only way he is going to be able to live in victory over fear, over worry, over sickness, or over poverty, is to delight in the Word of God. Then God's **Word** is going to become the most important thing in the world to you. God's Word is going to be your lifestream; God's Word is going to be your very prosperity, because you have tried all the natural ways; you have tried all the things you know to get free from fear, worry, confusion and disappointment; you've tried everything you know to get your family lined up, but it's just not working.

105

Therefore, you must come to the place where your delight is in the Word of God. If your delight is not in the Word of God, you are still trusting in the flesh. It is only the man whose delight is in the Word of God, who will meditate in it day and night. Because if you don't really delight in the Word, you have to fight and struggle to do it. If you will keep on fighting and struggling and doing it, praise God, it will come alive inside of you. But there will come a time when you will **delight** in the Word of God. There will come a time when you will be so excited to get through doing something else so you can study the Word. There will come a time in your life when the most important thing of your day will be to come to the place you can get your Bible out and begin to study the things of God. Delighting! Remember the times when you've had a hard day, and you come home and delight in lying back in your easy chair? Your wife fixes you a good meal, and it's a delight to you. Many times when you are tired at the end of a day you go home at night and slip down between the sheets, and it's a delight to you, just to lie there and relax. God wants you to know that He will bring you to the place your delight shall be in His Word and the things pertaining to that Word. When your delight is in God and the things of God, then you will desire to do them all the time. Have you ever noticed how a person gets caught up in something, let's say for example, playing pool? They delight in playing pool. Do you know what they do? Every time they get a chance they hunt for a pool table, because they delight in it! There is a place in Christ where your delight can be in the **Word of God**. Until your delight is in the law of the Lord, in the Word of God, you will not meditate upon it day and night. It will seem to be a struggle for you at first. You may have to battle and fight to meditate upon the Word. But God says He will bring you to the place where your delight shall be in the law of the Lord. The main reason Christians' delight is not in the law of the Lord is because they are not

106

really looking to God yet in some of these areas; they are still figuring how they are going to work it out themselves. Consistent meditation in the Word of God is necessary.

Joshua 1:8 says to meditate in His Word both day and night; why? "THAT THOU (or I) MAYEST BE ABLE TO DO ACCORDING TO ALL THAT IS WRITTEN." The reason many times Christians can't **do** according to the Word is because they have not meditated in it day and night; therefore, it hasn't become alive to them. That's why they can't act according to the Word.

Many times the reason you can't do something the Word says is because you haven't delighted in the Word; in other words, you haven't come to the place where you fell in love with it enough to really believe it. Really, that is the only way. As long as you think there is some other way besides the Word, then you are not really delighting in the Word. You have to come to the place where you realize there is only one way, and that's the Word way. The way of the Word! The way of the Cross; the way of Jesus Christ, the Son of God.

Knowledge in the head only, still produces death; it is of no spiritual value. You can take the Word of God and start meditating, and get it in your mind, and you have to do that; you must delight enough in the Word to meditate on it day and night. But as long as it is in your head only, it is still death. All you have is a head full of knowledge. All rivers run into the sea, but yet the sea never gets full. You can keep putting information into your mind, but it is necessary to get it in your heart. If you are going to maintain protection, and know that God's angels are there all the time, you can't meditate on protection once a week, once a month; because if you're trusting God's angels to keep you from having accidents, and if you're trusting God's Word to be healed, you know how often you're going to be meditating on it? **All the time.**

II. **CONSISTENT CONFESSION FOR FAITH**

OPERATION: There has to be consistent confession, for faith to operate. **Proverbs 2:10** says, "WHEN WISDOM ENTERETH INTO THINE HEART." Saints, in the heart is light, life, and power. It's only when the Word enters your heart that it is light, life, and power. As long as it is in your head (in the mind only), it is dry and barren and ineffective, with no practical life changing influence. When the Word has just stopped in your mind concerning protection, about angels, it is dry and ineffective. By the stripes of Jesus I am healed — that's life to me, that's light to me. That's a beam that is shining bright inside of me, because I have meditated on that so much that I have a body that is healthy and strong, based upon the Word of God. It is when it's in your hearts, saints, that it's life and light and power; that's when it beams out and the Word is pleasant to your soul. When the Word is just in your mind, it is not pleasant to your soul; you don't delight in it; you don't desire to feed upon it both day and night, because it is dry and barren. I can teach your mind, and you can educate your mind. But, glory to God, it is the work of the Holy Spirit of God to put it in your heart. That's why a man has to trust in God. Man can go just so far; I can help you just so far. But there comes a time when the Holy Spirit of God can reach down and put it in your heart, and it becomes life. When you hear it with your mind, it is just dry and barren; you hear it and it registers, but it doesn't really do anything for you. But when it hits your mind and then drops in your heart . . .! Something happens.

It is the man whose "DELIGHT IS IN THE LAW OF THE LORD" **(Psalm 1:1)** who is preserved from walking "IN THE COUNSEL OF THE UNGODLY." It is only the man who has the Word of God in his heart who can reject the counsel of the ungodly. If the Word is not in your heart, then the ungodly and the systems of the world can convince you to go their way. Whenever they talk you into going their way, recognize that the Word is in your head, and not your heart. When they can talk you into trusting in Blue Cross instead of the Old Rugged Cross, the Word is not in your heart. When you have the Word of God inside you, that by the stripes of Jesus you were healed, that the angels encamp round about you, the logic and reason of man's systems (the counsel of the ungodly) doesn't do anything but bounce off the walls. Some men think you are crazy; and the truth of it is, they are the ones who are deceived. They have more trust in man and man's methodology and man's ways than they do God's. I want you to know that God today is raising Him up an army of men and women who are going to believe Him. He has always had a people who would believe Him. He's always had a people that would stand upon His Word. Today, there are people who are believing the Word of God; and they are maintaining protection, they are maintaining health, they are maintaining prosperity, and the things of God.

We are considering getting the Word in your heart in order to maintain protection. When in the heart the Scripture is not just an external rule, but it is a preserving, keeping principle. The Word in your head about angels is just an external rule. The Word in your head about healing is just an external rule. The Word just in your head about protection, about not buying on credit; it is just an external rule. When it enters the heart the Scripture is not just external, but is a preserving, keeping principle. Once it was an object you searched for, but now found, it has a practical life changing influence and power in your life. When you are searching for the truth of the Word of God, with your mind, you are getting hold of the Word of God, you are searching for it; but once you find it, confess it day and night and it drops in your heart, then it has practical life changing influence. Then it becomes life, then it becomes pleasure. Then you love to eat it; then you like to taste of it; then you like to think it, because it has become a life changing principle in your life.

Unless the truth of the Word of God concerning angels becomes that way in your life, sometimes it may work and sometimes it won't. The same is true about every other area of God's Word.

God is the source of all things, and as God's people learn to walk and trust God, and God alone, and love Him with all their heart, and all their soul, and all their mind, the glory of God is going to come down. He is going to begin to move in their lives and it's going to become alive like it never has before. Then it's life changing, and it's a practical pleasure.

III. **STOP THINKING FEAR POSSIBILITIES OR SUPPOSITIONS:** The third thing you must do is stop thinking fear possibilities or suppositions, because when you start thinking about angels protecting you, you can't see them with your natural eye. You are going to start thinking about fear possibilities — well, what if? Well, just suppose, just suppose!! "Just suppose that your daughter broke her arm and the bone was sticking out, what would you do? Just suppose you had a cancer, what would you do?" Listen, saints, **any** time you trust God you are better off than trusting a man. I believe trying to believe God in doubt is better than having confidence in man.

Psalm 121:7 says, "THE LORD SHALL PRESERVE THEE FROM ALL EVIL." That statement written on this page, or written in your mind, will never change your life. It has to be written in your heart. It has to become a part of you; you have to eat it and digest it, until it becomes a part of you.

Psalm 34:7 says the Angel of the Lord encampeth round about me and delivereth me from destruction.

Psalm 91:11 says He has given His angels charge over us to deliver us, to keep us in all our ways, and to deliver us from evil.

James 4:7 says, "SUBMIT YOURSELVES THERE- FORE TO GOD. RESIST THE DEVIL, AND HE WILL FLEE FROM YOU." If you are going to move and maintain

110

protection, then you must stop thinking fear possibilities. You can't stop them from coming to your mind, but you can abort them. You can kill them, by quoting the Word of God, by submitting yourself to the Word of God, and saying, "THE **LORD** SHALL DELIVER ME FROM **EVERY** EVIL WORK" (II Timothy 4:18). You take your mind off the possibility (what **might** happen) and put your mind upon Scripture, upon the Word of God. The way you resist Satan is by holding fast to the Word. Hold fast your confession of faith, and he will flee from you.

IV. **STOP TALKING FEAR:** If you don't stop thinking fear, then you will not be able to stop talking fear. Words reflect the thoughts of the mind. It reveals to Satan his effectiveness. The words that come out of your mouth about possibilities — fear, accidents, robberies, death — as these words come out of your mouth they reveal what is in your mind. Your mouth will expose you. Stop talking fear; it reveals to Satan his effectiveness. You know how the devil knows if he is really working on you with fear? You tell him with your mouth. How does he know it's working unless you tell him? He'll never know you don't have victory over the fear of accidents unless you tell him.

When you talk fear you are giving the devil the O.K. to progress against you. Saints, when you go down and buy a protection policy (that the law doesn't make you buy), do you know what you are doing? You are saying, "I believe I may have an accident, so I'm protecting myself in case I do." When you buy that piece of paper the devil knows what you are saying. You are saying the possibility is there.

Let me give you another example, and I encourage you to search your heart about it. If you can't get rid of your insurance, what you are saying is you don't believe God can deliver you from **every evil work**; therefore, you have insurance **just in case** evil works come. If you can't get rid of your credit cards, do you know what you are saying? You are saying you've got to have them in order to make it.

Fear is Satan's weapon to birth doubt. This is how the devil births doubt in people — through fear. So what is the solution? Get the Word in your mind, get it in your heart. Stay with the Word until it becomes a life changing principle for you. Only then can you stop thinking fear. If you can't stop thinking fear, the fear will take hold of your mind and control you; and that means the knowledge was in your head and not your heart, because it hasn't changed your life.

V. **ACT IN WAYS THAT DEMONSTRATE TRUST AND CONFIDENCE IN GOD:** If you're going to maintain protection, you must act in ways that demonstrate your trust and confidence in God. **James 2:17** says faith without action is dead. Faith without corresponding action is dead. You can say all day long you trust God, but if your actions don't prove it, it's not there. You can say all day long you love God, but if you're not living a life totally dedicated to Jesus, you're a liar. What you mean is you're loving Him but you're wanting to tie Him **onto** your life; you don't want HIM **to be** your life; you want to do what you want to do and tie Him on the end of it. In order for divine protection to work, you'd better sell out to Jesus. Many people are going to be disappointed when they stand before the Master, and they walk before Him with all their policies in their little satchels, and all those stocks and bonds, and they say, "Jesus, we were looking for You to come any time." He says, "You were? And you've got your little brown satchel, and your safe deposit key jingling; buying and hoarding those stocks up?" "We were looking for You to come any time, Jesus. We were getting ready for You, Jesus." Truth is sharper than a two-edged sword; but it will set you free if you respond to it. Put God first and make Him the center of your life, and He says He will add everything else to you. Then God will bless you more than you've **ever** been blessed

112

before, because the Word will be life, and light, and power, dwelling inside of you. The Word of God will be the controlling principle in your life.

It is impossible to do points III and IV and V of this chapter, if you don't do points I and II. If you don't do the meditating and the confessing in your heart, you can't stop thinking, and stop talking, and stop acting fear.

Hebrews 11:6 says, "HE IS A REWARDER OF THEM THAT DILIGENTLY SEEK HIM."

Philippians 1:6 says, "BEING CONFIDENT OF THIS VERY THING, THAT HE WHICH HATH BEGUN A GOOD WORK IN YOU WILL PERFORM IT UNTIL THE DAY OF JESUS CHRIST." God has begun a good work in you concerning protection, as you have meditated on this study guide. Therefore, you can be confident He will do a good work. Let that Word begin to grow deep down inside you, and settle down inside you and take control of your life.

Hebrews 10:35-36 says, "CAST NOT AWAY THEREFORE YOUR CONFIDENCE, WHICH HATH GREAT RECOMPENCE OF REWARD (great promise of reward). FOR YE HAVE NEED OF PATIENCE, THAT, AFTER YE HAVE DONE THE WILL OF GOD, YE MIGHT RECEIVE THE PROMISE."

Isaiah 54:17 says, "NO WEAPON THAT IS FORMED AGAINST THEE SHALL PROSPER." God has assigned His angels charge over you to protect you, and take care of you in ALL your ways. For God's protection policy to work for you, it's based upon your paying the premium of having the Word in your heart. If you don't, then you void the protection policy. The Word must abide in your heart. You can have it, but you will have to pay the premium. You will have to meet the conditions. You will have to make up your mind. Decide to follow Jesus! It's not Jesus plus something else; it is putting Jesus first. Make up your mind who is Lord of your life, make up your mind what the controlling principle, the dominating center of your life is. What is the hub of your life? Are Jesus and His Word the hub and center of your life? Are you making everything that you think and do, everything that touches your life, conform to the hub, Jesus? Or are you trying to take Jesus and conform Him around your plans? It doesn't work that way.

The following is a prophetic utterance that came forth at the end of this message as it was taught:

"My Word is the pathway. Yea, it is marked clearly, saith God. Yea, it is there before thee; choose thee this day which way thou shalt walk, saith the Lord thy God. Choose ye this day what thou shalt take with thee; choose thee this day what thou shalt leave behind. But, yea, I say unto thee, there are places that you walk with Me where you can't take anything with you, saith God. Yea, the only way you can walk in those places is to walk with **Me**, saith the Lord. And I don't need any help, saith God. I don't need any extra weights, saith God. I don't need any extra luggage, saith God. So I say unto thee, choose thee; choose thee which way thou shalt go. Choose thee **this** day, saith the Lord thy God; because, yea, thou art mine, and I have called thee, saith God, to go with Me all the way. So it's **your** choice, it's **your** choice, it's **your** choice. Choose **Me**, and My way, and yea, the blessings of the Holy Spirit of the Living God shall **mushroom** forth out of thee and the anointing of God shall rise forth out of thee, and thou shalt be known as **My people**. Thou shalt be delightful in the land because thy testimony shall be bright and thy testimony shall be **clear**; and yea, those in

114

darkness shall come to the brightness of thy testimony, and they shall come and know **Me**, and they, too, shall choose to walk with Me. So walk a straight path, saith God. Walk with Me a **long** way, saith God, that you might lead others a long way, saith the Lord.''

Study Notes for
Protection by Angels

Study Notes for
Protection by Angels

Study Notes for
Protection by Angels

_____
_____
_____
_____
_____
_____
_____
_____
_____
_____
_____
_____
_____
_____
_____
_____
_____
_____
_____
_____
_____
_____
_____
_____
_____
_____
_____
_____
_____
_____
_____

Study Notes for
Protection by Angels

Study Notes for
Protection by Angels

Study Notes for
Protection by Angels

Study Notes for
Protection by Angels

_____

_____

_____

_____

_____

_____

_____

_____

_____

_____

_____

_____

_____

_____

_____

_____

_____

_____

_____

_____

_____

_____

_____

_____

_____

_____

_____

_____

Study Notes for
Protection by Angels